William Robinson Clark

Witnesses to Christ

A Contribution to Christian Apologetics

William Robinson Clark

Witnesses to Christ
A Contribution to Christian Apologetics

ISBN/EAN: 9783337167356

Printed in Europe, USA, Canada, Australia, Japan

Cover: Foto ©Lupo / pixelio.de

More available books at **www.hansebooks.com**

The Baldwin Lectures, 1887

WITNESSES TO CHRIST

A CONTRIBUTION
TO
CHRISTIAN APOLOGETICS

WILLIAM CLARK, M.A.
PROFESSOR OF PHILOSOPHY IN TRINITY COLLEGE, TORONTO

CHICAGO
A. C. McCLURG AND COMPANY
1888

COPYRIGHT,
BY A. C. MCCLURG AND CO.
A.D. 1888.

EXTRACT FROM THE DEED OF TRUST,

IN ACCORDANCE WITH THE PROVISIONS OF WHICH THE BALDWIN LECTURES WERE INSTITUTED.

"This Instrument, made and executed between Samuel Smith Harris, Bishop of the Protestant Episcopal Church in the Diocese of Michigan, of the city of Detroit, Wayne County, Michigan, as party of the first part, and Henry P. Baldwin, Alonzo B. Palmer, Henry A. Hayden, Sidney D. Miller, and Henry P. Baldwin, 2d, of the State of Michigan, Trustees under the trust created by this instrument, as parties of the second part, witnesseth as follows : —

"In the year of Our Lord one thousand eight hundred and eighty-five, the said party of the first part, moved by the importance of bringing all practicable Christian influences to bear upon the great body of students annually assembled at the University of Michigan, undertook to promote and set in operation a plan of Christian work at said University, and collected contributions for that purpose, of which plan the following outline is here given, that is to say : —

"1. To erect a building or hall near the University,

in which there should be cheerful parlors, a well-equipped reading-room, and a lecture-room where the lectures hereinafter mentioned might be given;

" 2. To endow a lectureship similar to the Bampton Lectureship in England, for the establishment and defence of Christian truth: the lectures on such foundation to be delivered annually at Ann Arbor by a learned clergyman or other communicant of the Protestant Episcopal Church, to be chosen as hereinafter provided: such lectures to be not less than six nor more than eight in number, and to be published in book form before the income of the fund shall be paid to the lecturer;

" 3. To endow two other lectureships, one on Biblical Literature and Learning, and the other on Christian Evidences: the object of such lectureships to be to provide for all the students who may be willing to avail themselves of them a complete course of instruction in sacred learning, and in the philosophy of right thinking and right living, without which no education can justly be considered complete;

" 4. To organize a society, to be composed of the students in all classes and departments of the University who may be members of or attached to the Protestant Episcopal Church, of which society the Bishop of the Diocese, the Rector, Wardens, and Vestrymen of St. Andrew's Parish, and all the Professors of the University who are communicants of the Protestant Episcopal Church should be members *ex officio*, which society should have the care and management of the reading-room and lecture-room of the hall, and of all exercises or employments carried on therein, and should moreover annually elect each of the lecturers hereinbefore mentioned, upon the nomination of the Bishop of the Diocese.

"In pursuance of the said plan, the said society of students and others has been duly organized under the name of the 'Hobart Guild of the University of Michigan;' the hall above mentioned has been builded and called 'Hobart Hall;' and Mr. Henry P. Baldwin of Detroit, Michigan, and Sibyl A. Baldwin, his wife, have given to the said party of the first part the sum of ten thousand dollars for the endowment and support of the lectureship first hereinbefore mentioned.

"Now, therefore, I, the said Samuel Smith Harris, Bishop as aforesaid, do hereby give, grant, and transfer to the said Henry P. Baldwin, Alonzo B. Palmer, Henry A. Hayden, Sidney D. Miller, and Henry P. Baldwin, 2d, Trustees as aforesaid, the said sum of ten thousand dollars to be invested in good and safe interest-bearing securities, the net income thereof to be paid and applied from time to time as hereinafter provided, the said sum and the income thereof to be held in trust for the following uses: —

"1. The said fund shall be known as the Endowment Fund of the Baldwin Lectures.

"2. There shall be chosen annually by the Hobart Guild of the University of Michigan, upon the nomination of the Bishop of Michigan, a learned clergyman or other communicant of the Protestant Episcopal Church, to deliver at Ann Arbor and under the auspices of the said Hobart Guild, between the Feast of St. Michael and All Angels and the Feast of St. Thomas, in each year, not less than six nor more than eight lectures, for the Establishment and Defence of Christian Truth; the said lectures to be published in book form by Easter of the following year, and to be entitled 'The Baldwin Lectures;' and there shall be paid to the said lecturer the income of the said endowment fund, upon the delivery of fifty copies of said lectures to the said Trustees or their successors; the said printed volumes to contain, as an extract from this instrument, or in condensed form, a statement of the object and conditions of this trust."

PREFACE.

IT is needless to say that the lectures published in this volume were undertaken and delivered under a very deep sense of responsibility, and even with a measure of anxiety. If this anxiety was excessive, I may plead that it is a serious matter to deal with the phases of contemporaneous thought in their relation to the truth of the Gospel, and to endeavor to extort testimonies to the power of the Cross from foes as well as from friends. It is a serious undertaking " to contend earnestly for the faith which was once for all delivered unto the saints."

Whether this work has been accomplished with any kind of success, it does not become me to say. I may, however, be permitted to remark that I have not addressed myself to the subjects of these lectures without having taken considerable pains to become acquainted with the positions of our opponents; and further, that I shall have reason to be amply satisfied if the public shall receive the volume with only a fair measure of the kind acceptance granted to the lectures when they were delivered.

"We owe these foundations,"[1]—the "Hobart Guild" and the "Baldwin Lectures,"—says my distinguished and accomplished predecessor, Bishop Cleveland Coxe, "to the enlightened wisdom and foresight of the Right Reverend Prelate, who, with such great advantage to the Church at large, now presides over the Diocese of Michigan. But he would hardly forgive me should I neglect to add, that in the munificence of Governor Baldwin and his accomplished wife he has found that sort of encouragement and help without which the ablest and most zealous bishop is impotent to effect what his heart and head may prompt him to propose as due alike to the Republic and to the Church of Christ."

It was of unspeakable advantage to the second lecturer that the importance of the work of the Guild should have been commended by Bishop Cleveland Coxe, although in other respects it made his own work more difficult. It is impossible for me to say how greatly my task was lightened by the generous support of the Bishop of Michigan, by whom I was appointed to the lectureship with the hearty concurrence

---

[1] The reader is referred more particularly to the extract from the "Deed of Trust" on page 5.

of Governor Baldwin. The people of Detroit and of the Diocese of Michigan know these illustrious men too well to need that a comparative stranger should do more than express his personal gratitude and respect for them.

It is seldom, perhaps, in the preface to lectures of this kind, that remarks of a character so personal should be introduced. But it is hardly possible to do otherwise at the beginning of such an undertaking; and I shelter myself under the great example of my predecessor when I acknowledge the personal kindness and sympathy which I received from the inhabitants of the beautiful university town in which the lectures were delivered.

To several of the Professors, to private members of the Episcopal Church, and to prominent representatives of other communions, I am under deep and lasting obligations. To the Rev. Dr. Earp, Rector of St. Andrew's Church, who has done such admirable and successful work for the Episcopal Church and for the Hobart Guild, not only my thanks but the thanks of the whole community are due, and are here offered by me in my own name, and in the name of many besides myself.

In a course of lectures, the material for which has been accumulating through a number of years, it is not easy to indicate all the sources from which ideas or trains of thought have been derived. Wherever I have known of any obligations of this kind I have acknowledged them in the notes, although doubtless many have escaped my memory. With reference to the two lectures on the Resurrection, it may seem a matter of surprise that no reference is made to Dr. Milligan's excellent work on this subject. The fact is, that these lectures were drawn up immediately after the publication of the third volume of " Supernatural Religion," and before I had seen Dr. Milligan's work. Whatever coincidences may be found, are attributable simply to our having dealt with the same subject and the same material.

May our gracious and loving Lord accept this humble tribute to the truth and glory of His work, and pardon its defects!

W. C.

TRINITY COLLEGE, TORONTO,
 Epiphany, 1888.

CONTENTS.

LECTURE I.

PHASES AND FAILURES OF UNBELIEF.

PAGE

Reasons for Unbelief. — Conflict to be expected. — The Work of the Church in the Past. — Present Duty. — The Spirit of our Work. — The present Position of the Conflict. — Fears and Hopes. — The last Hundred Years. — Three Phases of Thought in Unbelief: the Theological, the Metaphysical, and the Positive. — Apparent Discouragements. — The Three Forms of Unbelief: I. RATIONALISM, — Reimarus; Paulus; Examples of Treatment; Uses; Failure. II. MYTHICISM, — Strauss, Value of his Work, gave a Death-blow to Rationalism; Measure of Truth in Pantheism; Failure of Mythicism; Renan's "Vie de Jésus;" Strauss's new "Leben Jesu." III. MATERIALISM, — Strauss's "The Old Faith and the New" . . . 19–49

LECTURE II.

CIVILIZATION AND CHRISTIANITY.

The Gospel in the World. — Christian Ideal and Christian Life contrasted. — Has Christianity failed? — Modern Civilization and Christianity. — Opposing Views. — I. The World before Christ: Claims of the Ancient World real; Serious Defects; vitiated by Egoism. — Plato and Aristotle. — Citizens, Slaves, Barbarians, Enemies. — Greeks and Romans alike. — Cicero. — Condition of various Classes: 1. Women, — Status, Marriage, Dependence; 2. Working Classes, — Manual

Labor thought degrading; 3. Slaves, — Slavery accepted by the Philosophers, the Laws relating to Slavery, Slavery in Practice, Exceptions, Doctrine of Stoics. — II. The Need supplied: the Gospel of Human Brotherhood; its Foundation in Christ. — The Kingdom of God; its Subjects; its Laws. — Changes effected: 1. Condition of Women; 2. Laboring Classes; 3. The Poor, — provided for by Christianity; the Emperor Julian; 4. Slaves, — Objection that there is no Christian Command for Emancipation; Answer, — what the Gospel has done, what it has to do; 5. War; 6. Legislation. — Conclusion 50–78

LECTURE III.

PERSONAL CULTURE AND RELIGION.

Man, Individual and Social. — Transition from Civilization to personal Culture. — Man's Nature and Culture. — Points of Agreement. — I. Theories of Culture various, but reducible to two, Religious and Non-Religious: 1. The Non-Religious, — (1) Social, (2) Scientific, (3) Literary, (4) Positivist; 2. The Christian. — II. Means of Attainment: Human Culture not undervalued, but insufficient, as not taking account of Man's whole Nature; illustrated: 1. Idea of Immortality; 2. Responsibility, — (1) Conscience, (2) the Idea of God, (3) Consciousness of Sin, (4) how met by the Gospel, (5) Effects produced. — Mill. — Goethe and Saint François de Sales. — Luther and Rousseau. — General Effects. — The Christian Ideal. — Lecky. — Mill on Belief in Immortality; on the Life and Teaching of Jesus. 79–113

LECTURE IV.

THE UNITY OF CHRISTIAN DOCTRINE.

Does the Bible teach definite Religious Truth? — Denied. — What may be meant by the Denial? — Divine Revelation in Christ. — Gradually unfolded. — True De-

velopment. — Illustrated in the Writings of Saint Paul.
— Later Examples of Development in the History of
the Church. — Schools of Thought. — Development
and Accretion distinguished. — Illustrations of Unity
in Christian Teaching : 1. The Nature of God. — Represented as possessing Human Attributes and as being
far removed from Humanity. — Deistic and Pantheistic
Conceptions. — 2. The Character of God. — Divine
Decrees and Human Liberty. — 3. The Nature of Man.
— Original Sin. — Concupiscence. — 4. Eschatology. —
Future Retribution. — Three current Theories. — Not
absolutely Irreconcilable. — Analogy of the Book of
Nature and Science with the Book of Grace and
Theology 114-141

LECTURE V.

THE INSUFFICIENCY OF MATERIALISM.

Universality of Belief in God. — Materialism and Atheism
inseparably connected. — Materialism, what it is. — Materialistic Accounts of the Origin of Life. — Evolution
not necessarily materialistic. — The Atomic Theory no
Explanation of Life. — Materialism, pure and simple,
generally abandoned. — Opinions of eminent Scientific
Men. — The Principle of Energy or Force. — Mr. Spencer's Exposition. — Must we not go further? Mr.
Spencer, to some Extent, in Agreement with the Gospel,
— but in his "Force" we recognize Mind. — We are
compelled to go beyond the Facts and Laws of the
Material Universe. — We know Mind directly, Matter
indirectly. — What do we learn from the External
World ? — Kant's Categories. — Laws of Nature imply Mind. — The Argument from Design, — Objections considered. — What we believe and assert. —
Our Conclusions called in Question. — Spirit personal.
— The Ego and Non-Ego. — The Analogy of the Finite
inapplicable to the Infinite. — Conclusions . . . 142-179

LECTURE VI.

THE PESSIMISM OF THE AGE.

PAGE

Connection between Faith and Action. — Different Tendencies in Human Nature explain the Origin of Pessimism and Optimism. — Meaning of these Terms. — Views of Jews, Greeks, and Romans. — Christian View. — Sentiment of Deism. — Buddhism. — I. Modern Pessimism, — Leopardi, Schopenhauer, Hartmann; Leopardi's three possible Ways of Happiness; Schopenhauer's Theory. — II. What we are to think of Pessimism. — 1. Effort not necessarily productive of Unhappiness; 2. Pleasure not merely Negative; 3. The Development and Elevation of Life not a mere Increase of Misery. — Increased Sensibility and Intelligence also a Source of Happiness. — Testimonies of Instinct and Reason. — The Reply of Pessimism: Men deceive themselves. — The Rejoinder of Consciousness. — A Future Life. — III. How can we account for Pessimism? — Partly the Result of Temperament and Constitution, partly of the Circumstances of Individuals and Communities. — Chief Cause found in the State of Religious Belief. — Condition of Germany. — Pessimism can flourish only on the Ruins of Faith. — Examples of Faith and Unbelief. — The Gospel and Agnosticism. — Deism. — Atheism. — Pessimism the last Word of Positivism. — Conclusion 180–215

LECTURE VII.

THE RESURRECTION OF JESUS CHRIST.

PART I.

EXAMINATION OF THE EVIDENCE FOR THE RESURRECTION.

1. Introductory. — Importance of the Event. — The Gospel founded on Facts. — Necessity of Revelation for the Support of Religious Truth. — 2. The Fact of the Resurrection. — Its Meaning. — 3. The Nature of the Evidence. — No Evidence sufficient for those who dis-

believe in the Supernatural. — The Existence of a Personal God postulated. — The Church exists and professes to have the Knowledge of God by Revelation. — The Burden of Proof not entirely with the Christian. — Points on which there is general Agreement. — The Documentary Proof. — Two Questions : (1) What did the Disciples of Christ believe? (2) Are we justified in believing the Same? — 4. The Evidence of the Gospel Histories; their Agreement; their Statements. — Objections : Not seen to rise; Disagreement as to the Time, as to the Circumstances; Legendary Details. — Answers. — Final Verdict on Evidence. — 5. The Evidence of Saint Paul. — Documents admitted. — Points of Agreement. — What the admitted Documents assert. — An independent Testimony. — Its Value affected by the Character of the Witness. — Objections to his Testimony. — Answers. — The Value of Saint Paul's Testimony. — Disingenuous and inconsistent Objection. — Answer 216–254

LECTURE VIII.

THE RESURRECTION OF JESUS CHRIST.

PART II.

EXAMINATION OF THEORIES INVENTED TO SET ASIDE THE EVIDENCE FOR THE RESURRECTION.

No Evidence will convince those who are resolved not to believe. — Theory of Imposture abandoned. — How, then, escape from the Force of the Testimony? — Two Theories: 1. The Theory of Apparent Death, — partly abandoned, partly kept in Reserve. — The one Element of Probability in the Theory. — But consider what the Theory requires us to believe. — Difficulties. — Does not account for the Change in the Apostles. — Involves Imposture. — 2. The Vision Hypothesis. — The last Word of the Assailants. — Asserts Illusion, not Imposture. — The Theory explained. — Not entirely new. — Different Views of Strauss. — What the Illusion Theory involves. — Requires the inadmissible Assumption that the Disciples expected the Resurrection. — The Theory does not account for the Change in the Disciples. — Inconsistent Treatment of the Gospels. — Mary Magdalene. — The Apostles. — Their Doubts and Disbelief. — The Vision fails to account for undoubted Facts. — Why did the Appearances cease so abruptly? — What became of the Sacred Body? — The Truth of the Resurrection alone accounts for the new Faith of the Disciples. — The End of this Controversy 255–285

Notes 287–300

WITNESSES TO CHRIST.

LECTURE I.

PHASES AND FAILURES OF UNBELIEF.

Reasons for Unbelief. — Conflict to be expected. — The Work of the Church in the Past. — Present Duty. — The Spirit of our Work. — The present Position of the Conflict. — Fears and Hopes. — The last Hundred Years. — Three Phases of Thought in Unbelief: the Theological, the Metaphysical, and the Positive. — Apparent Discouragements. — The Three Forms of Unbelief: I. RATIONALISM, — Reimarus; Paulus; Examples of Treatment; Uses; Failure. II. MYTHICISM, — Strauss, Value of his Work, gave a Death-blow to Rationalism; Measure of Truth in Pantheism; Failure of Mythicism; Renan's "Vie de Jésus;" Strauss's new "Leben Jesu." III. MATERIALISM, — Strauss's "The Old Faith and the New."

IF the Gospel is true, why is it not generally, or even universally, believed and accepted? If it is really a message of salvation sent from God to His sinful creatures who have sore need of it, how is it that it is not welcomed by the sinful, — how is it that it is disbelieved, rejected, opposed? Such questions are often asked by Christians and by unbelievers alike, — by the latter scornfully, triumphantly; by the former sorrowfully, despondently. By the one and the other it seems to be assumed that a message that was true and beneficent must find a ready acceptance.

And yet those who know and remember the words of the Lord Jesus are aware that He did not expect the world to yield at once to His authority and His claims. Although at His birth the heavenly hosts proclaimed peace on earth; although he left with His disciples the blessing of peace which the world could not give, and which no man could take away from them; although His very name was the Prince of Peace, yet He told them that He came not to send peace upon earth, but a sword; and He who takes the sword must smite with the sword, and either perish by the sword, or by it gain a lasting victory and triumph. This conflict has gone on ever since the Lord of life was lifted up into His throne of glory; and all His faithful followers must be like Him, their Lord, who is "a man of war," and must fight the good fight of faith even unto death.

It is a great and a terrible warfare to which we are called, — to take part in that great battle of Armageddon which has been raging ever since moral evil appeared in the universe, and with respect to which no neutrality is allowed, since a curse is spoken against those who stand by and come not "to the help of the Lord against the mighty." And it is a fight which must be fought with no weapons of earthly fashioning or of earthly temper, but with those which are taken from the armory of heaven and are sanctioned by the Leader of the hosts of heaven.

"Ye shall bear witness," said Christ to His Apostles; and this is one chief duty, we might say the first of all the duties which are laid upon the Church of Christ in the world, and upon every member of it, that they should be witnesses for God, — witnesses against sin and error, witnesses for goodness and truth, letting their light so shine before men that they may see their good works, and glorify their Father which is in heaven.

In many different ways and in many different circumstances must this testimony be borne; and although in one sense it is ever the same, yet there is need of constant vigilance, wisdom, readiness, that it may be a word spoken in season as it is needed, doing for men that special work which their necessities require and demand, and which God thus indicates as the work which He expects His people to perform. Thus He wills that wherever our lot is cast, we shall "earnestly contend for the faith once delivered to the saints."

It can hardly be charged against the Church that she has ever wholly forgotten this duty. Sometimes her enemies have come in the form of that brutal violence which sought to crush and destroy her life; sometimes under the subtle garb of sophistry, which really aimed at the destruction of her testimony to the truth as it is in Jesus, while it seemed to be endeavoring to help its progress; sometimes in the form of unbelief, — at one time calm, rational, and philosophical in tone; or again, biting, sarcastic, and contemptuous. But against all of these adversaries the Church has, with varying faith and power, with varying courage and hopefulness, and so with varying success, carried on the conflict on behalf of her Lord and His truth. It could never be lawful for her to desist; for that which she conserved was not her own, but the bequest of Another, and she had no choice but to defend and preserve it. And the same duty is handed on to ourselves, to contend not for anything which we can claim as our own, but for the honor of our God and the blessedness of His creatures.

And surely we must feel, if there is any conflict, if there is any duty, which requires of us that we should be wise as serpents and harmless as doves, it is this fighting for and defending the ark of God. For our antagonists are not our enemies. They are men who are loved by God; they are men for whom Christ died. They are men not to be treated with scorn and contumely, even though they may scorn us and blaspheme the holy name by which we are called; they are to be loved, pitied, prayed for, persuaded, reasoned with. In this spirit, and in no other, is it lawful for the servants of Jesus Christ to go forth against the enemies of the Cross.

It is one of the great glories of Christ, that, while He never lowers his own pretensions or His claims, He will not deny or question the rights of His creatures. He will have us reverence mankind, even when it is in error, because He will win men by truth and by love. Who are they that come forth to do battle against the Incarnate Word of God? Some there are, moved by the Spirit of Christ Himself, eager for a knowledge of truth, yet for a season blinded by prejudice, by ignorance, by influences the power of which they have not learned to overcome. Must we not pity such, and love them and be patient with them? And if there are others who have no real love of truth, who are held by the power of darkness and of Satan, alas! are not they even more to be pitied, if they are also to be blamed and rebuked? And if it is our duty at times to rebuke them sharply, surely it should be done in a spirit of meekness and lowliness, remembering who it is that hath made us to differ. God help us thus to meet the enemies of the Cross as those who hope that one day we may clasp their hands as friends! May we not also remind ourselves of that truth which will again and again force itself upon our attention in the course of our inquiry, — that we have much to learn, and that we have actually learned much from the attacks and criticisms of our adversaries?

Every age has its own peculiar difficulties in dealing with unbelief; and it is not wonderful that each age should see the special arduousness of its own appointed work. Doubtless there are in our own days peculiar dangers and discouragements in connection with the work of maintaining the faith; but there are also peculiar helps and elements of hopefulness lying side by side with these very difficulties. Let us try to understand the position of the armies of faith and unbelief, and we shall see that these words are not spoken without reason.

One of the most subtle as well as offensive modes of assailing the faith is the method adopted by those who talk in a patronizing manner of the benefits which religion has conferred upon mankind in earlier and ruder ages, while they deny that it is any longer a necessity for the human race. Religion, in their view, has had its day. It was useful, they think, in the early stages of human civilization, when the laws of Nature were comparatively unknown, and men could not be influenced by intelligent self-interest. Then, the thought of a Being whose commands men were bound to obey, who could reward them for their obedience and punish them for their disobedience, was useful and helpful; but now it would be a distinct hindrance to a clear discernment of the laws and true conditions of human life. And these are the conclusions of perhaps no inconsiderable number of educated and reflecting men in our own days. We cannot wonder that many believers in Divine Revelation should be seriously disquieted, and that some should even be greatly alarmed, at the progress of such opinions.

It would be unreasonable for the Christian apologist to ignore this somewhat altered state of things. It would be foolish to infer, that, because religion seems to make great progress in these later days, therefore all opposition to it must speedily cease, or may be safely ignored. The warfare between faith and unbelief will never cease until the end shall come. It cannot be said with truth that the fight is hotter than in former days. On the contrary, it is cooler, calmer, carried on with less of noise and of passion; but it is as deep and as earnest as ever. It is perhaps natural that this superficial change should have come over the spirit of the combatants. The exact nature of the conflict is much better known. Men are no longer fighting in the dark or in the twilight, but in clear day. They are no longer in such danger of confounding friends and foes, of striking out wildly because they are in partial ignorance of their position and circumstances. The field of battle is more clearly marked out; the position of the enemy is more accurately determined. Both sides know much better the exact nature of the work to be done.

Most persons will agree that such a state of things is more satisfactory in every way; and those who believe in the truth of Divine Revelation will consider it as hopeful for the cause of truth. But it is not so much in this circumstance that we discern the brighter prospects which the present offers us, but rather in the fact that unbelief has now run its course and exhausted all its armory in its assaults upon the faith. To the statement that religion has had its day, and must now pass away and give place to natural knowledge, we oppose the assertion that unbelief has had its day; that it has tried one weapon after another against the walls of the City of God, and that not one of them has prospered; that they have so visibly failed that one after another has been cast away, and that there remains nothing for those who would continue the assault, but the use of arms which have already been found ineffectual, and which have been. already rejected as useless by the soldiers of the army of unbelief.

We go further. When we review the past history of the criticism that has sought to undermine the foundations of Divine Revelation, we not only behold the evidences of victory to the cause of truth, but we see that the Church has learned much and gained much in the conflict. We find out, what we might have anticipated if we had been wiser, that every form of error which has opposed itself to the faith of Christ has either contained some precious germ of truth, or has over against it some partial error which has attached itself to certain representations of the faith.

It was a wise remark of a French Bishop, that we must not hurl anathemas at the natural order, and that we must respect human reason at the same time that we make it feel its weakness and its impotence. We believe that this is one of the most valuable lessons that are impressed upon us by the past history of unbelief. If it has shown us its weakness and the weakness of its origin, it has also taught us to discover some of our own weaknesses and errors. If it has shattered itself against the fortifications which it sought in vain to destroy, it has left among the heaps of rubbish which are strewn around the City of God some precious jewels which may be set in the walls of the heavenly Jerusalem.

During the past hundred years the history of unbelief has passed through three distinct phases, corresponding with Comte's three stages of human thought,—the theological, the metaphysical, and the positive. In adopting this period as the nearest to our own times, it is by no means intended to be implied that the same lessons are not deducible from other periods of Christian history. The whole history of unbelief in all ages partakes of the same changing and uncertain character. But there is a special advantage in selecting a period which can be surveyed without any considerable difficulty, — a period in which the modes of thought correspond more nearly with our own than those by which earlier ages were characterized, and the changes of which can be grasped and exhibited with comparative ease.

These three stages,[1] then, — the theological, the metaphysical, and the positive, — represent the different phases of unbelief, from the publication of the "Wolfenbüttel Fragments"[2] (a convenient starting-point), in 1778, to the present day. Let us remember that these fragments appeared in their complete form forty years after the publication of Butler's "Analogy" (1736); that they were being issued at the time of the death of David Hume, when the English unbeliever Thomas Paine (1737–1809) was about forty years of age, and about twenty years before the publication of Paley's "Evidences of Christianity" (1794). It might seem, at first sight, that a review of this period, extending over the last century, would be far from encouraging, when we remember that each stage in the progress of unbelief has manifested a more deadly hostility to the basis of the faith of Christ — that

---

[1] For some of these remarks I think I am indebted to a pamphlet by Dr. A. Schweizer which I no longer possess.

[2] See Note A.

is to say, to a belief in the supernatural — than the period by which it was preceded. But we shall certainly find, on a deeper consideration of the subject, that this progress in antagonism has, on the one hand, been a confession of weakness, and, on the other hand, has necessitated the taking up of positions which are less and less capable of being maintained.

If deism and rationalism gave place to pantheism and the mythical hypothesis; if these in their turn gave way to positivism, materialism, sheer atheism, — it has been because the earlier positions could not be defended. But we believe that the last battle-field chosen by unbelief offers it the least favorable vantage-ground of all; and it is in this circumstance that we venture to discover a ground of hope in looking forward to the future conflicts of the faith with unbelief.

I. Let us now try to understand the three forms of unbelief which have, during the last century, assailed the truth of the Gospel. The first was the *rationalistic;* and it was, for the most part, employed by those who were called deists. This form of error, in any wide sense, had its birthplace in England and in France, not in Germany. We are so accustomed to speak of German rationalism (and there have been many German rationalists in the past and in the present), that we are apt to forget that the Germans, as a nation, are not natively or distinctively rationalistic. Still, they worked out the theories which were transplanted from other countries, more particularly by Reimarus in the "Wolfenbüttel Fragments" already mentioned.

The most powerful German exponent of this theory was Paulus, who applied it first to the exposition of the Gospels, and afterwards more particularly to the explanation of the life of our Lord.[1] The distinctive character of the rationalistic theory was this, — that the Gospel stories were regarded as substantially historical, but in no case as having a supernatural character. The last is, of course, the one point of agreement between these various schools, — that they all exclude a belief in supernatural agency. This assumption lies at the foundation of each new theory, and is the explanation of its origin.

It was quite natural that the rationalistic theory should be the first in modern times as in ancient. It is difficult, as one reads the Gospel story, to believe that the events which are there described never took place. Even at a later period than that to which we are now referring, the sense of their historical reality has been forced upon unwilling minds. When M. Renan went to visit the Holy Land, before writing his "Vie de Jésus," he was under the influence of the mythical theory. But the testimony of the soil of Palestine was too strong for

---

[1] His "Commentary on the Gospels" appeared in 1800; his "Life of Jesus" (*Leben Jesu*), in 1828.

him. He felt, as he looked on the Galilean hills and stood by the Lake of Gennesareth, that in the Gospels he had to do with history. And so Paulus and his school say the events of the Gospel did take place, but they were purely natural, because there is no such thing, and there can be no such thing, as a miracle. This, we must repeat, is the one assumption (we had almost said the necessary assumption) of every school of unbelief; and the problem which each professes to solve is to account for the form of the stories which are found in the New Testament without admitting the notion of the supernatural as an explanation of their contents.

Let us take some examples of the rationalistic treatment of the Gospel history, and we shall better understand its methods and its difficulties. Take the first miracle, the provision of wine at the marriage of Cana in Galilee. Something of the kind, the rationalist would say, actually did take place; but there was no miracle wrought. According to Paulus,[1] the marriage took place in a poor family. It was probably foreseen that their provision would be insufficient, and it was a kindly jest on the part of Jesus and His friends to assist this poor family without hurting their feelings, and so they brought wine with them and introduced it

[1] It is with regret that we mention that Bunsen does not greatly differ from him. See his "Bibelwerk," Saint John, chap. ii.

in some such way as is described in the Gospel. So, with respect to the mightiest miracle of all, the resurrection of Jesus Christ, something of the kind actually took place, probably two or three days after the burial. He came out of the grave in which His body had been laid. But then He had not really been dead; He was only in a trance and had revived.

In the good providence of God — and here we are helped to understand how these assaults upon the faith are permitted — it came to pass that rationalism, with all its shallowness and insufficiency, contributed something to Christian thought. It compelled men to think of God as a Being who governed by law. It raised a serious protest against the notion that man's life and the affairs of the world were ordered by an arbitrary or a capricious will. We do not mean that these notions found the slightest justification in Holy Scripture, or in any of the authoritative teachings of the Church. But there had been, in the ordinary Christian teaching of the period, a too copious use of language which might seem to sanction theories so baseless; and it was a benefit to religion that men should be compelled to see in the laws of Nature, working regularly and harmoniously, rules of the eternal Divine intelligence.

As a positive system, or as a criticism of Divine revelation, however, rationalism broke down at all points. It was arbitrary and inconsistent in its method, and it furnished no real explanation of the facts for which it professed to account. When it is said that it accepted in substance the *facts* of the Gospels, but discarded the *opinions* of the writers, it overlooked the consideration that no writers have ever stated facts more simply, have ever introduced less of their own reflections into the narrative of the facts. When rationalism professed to believe that such things happened as are recorded in the Gospels, but that they were susceptible of a natural explanation, it abandoned the very principle which made the facts intelligible, and which explained the influence which they exerted on those who witnessed them.

The most striking illustration of the utter failure of the rationalistic hypothesis to explain the sacred narrative is found in its criticism of the resurrection of Christ; and this topic will receive careful consideration when it comes under special survey in the last of these lectures. But it began to be felt that it failed entirely to explain the power and influence of the life and work of Jesus Christ upon the men of his own age. If the rationalistic explanation were the true one, it was impossible to acquit the central Person in those transactions of the charge of imposture; and the day had gone by when such a suspicion could be entertained.

The difficulty of rationalism, and of the deism with which it has generally been associated, has been that it has gone too far or not far enough. The rationalists were mostly deists; and after all, a personal God is a supernatural fact, and unless we decide to expel Him from the government of the universe, He will be as great a difficulty in the world as He is in the Bible. It was this conviction, Mr. J. S. Mill tells us, that made him abandon deism and become an atheist. Butler, he says,[1] convinced him that every objection that could be urged against the difficulties of Christianity was equally applicable to the Divine government of the world.

II. Two causes prepared the way for the *mythical theory* of Strauss, — the failure of the rationalistic explanation, and the growth of a pantheistic habit of thought which had for long been at work undermining the prevalent deism. Neither Paulus nor Strauss originated either of the theories which are generally connected with their names. The principles which Paulus applied with more completeness than had hitherto been attempted to the life of our Lord had, as we have seen, been set forth in substance in the "Wolfenbüttel Fragments" many years before, and at a still earlier period by the English Deists. So the germ of the mythical theory of Strauss had been contained in the teachings of more than one of the disciples of Kant; and it had been employed by Eichhorn and De Wette to

---

[1] Three Essays on Religion, and Autobiography.

explain the contents of the Old Testament. It was reserved for Strauss to apply it unflinchingly to the Gospel narrative of the life of our Lord.

We must not withhold a certain degree of sympathy from the spirit which gave rise to the mythical theory. Its revulsion from the rationalistic method was wholesome, but it was not new. Fichte, who was only a year younger than Paulus,[1] had long before expressed a feeling which had become general as to the freethinking which is identical with rationalism. "The empty and unedifying chatter of the freethinkers," he said, "has had time enough to explain itself completely. It has explained itself, and we have heard it; and it has nothing new and nothing better to say than what it has already said. We are weary of it; we feel its emptiness and complete nullity when it comes in relation to our sense of the Eternal,—a sense which is inextinguishable, and which compels us to seek an object for it to rest upon."[2] Many such protests had been uttered against the rationalistic theory, but it was Strauss who gave it its death-blow.

Nor can we altogether withhold our sympathy from that pantheistic movement of which the theory of Strauss was the most remarkable

---

[1] J. G. Fichte was born in 1762.
[2] See Pfleiderer's "Religionsphilosophie" (Berlin, 1878), p. 72; English translation of later edition (London, 1886), vol. i. p. 286.

outcome. It is quite true that, critically and intellectually, pantheism is simple atheism; it is equally true that it commonly ends in formal atheism. But it is not always, or indeed often, at first atheistic in its temper or in its purpose. Nay, on the contrary, it contained and asserted a weighty truth concerning Almighty God which was ignored by the ordinary deism, and even sometimes by the popular orthodox theism, that "in Him we live, and move, and have our being." God had been regarded too much as a Being not merely distinct from the material creation, but external to it and apart from it, — to use philosophical language, as merely transcendent, and not also immanent. Pantheism bore witness to His immanence, if it ignored His transcendence. It declared the truth that He is the Life of all life, — not only the Beginner, but the living and life-giving and life-sustaining Preserver of all existence.

This was, of course, no new doctrine. It had been taught plainly in the Bible; it had been taught, to go back no further, in its pantheistic form, — that is, with the ignoring and denial of the Divine Personality, — by Spinoza. It was put forth by Herder (1744-1803) as a protest against the religious philosophy of Kant and his first followers. "The first error ($\pi\rho\hat{\omega}\tau o\nu$ $\psi\epsilon\hat{v}\delta o\varsigma$) in your system," wrote Herder to Jacobi, "and in that of all the opponents of Spinoza, is this: that God, as the great Substance of all substances, is a nonentity, a mere abstract idea. He is not this, according to Spinoza, but the ever-working One, who alone can say to Himself, 'I am who am, and shall be in all the variations of My manifestations what I shall be.' What you, dear people, mean by your 'Existence external to the world,' I do not understand."[1]

When we are proving the unsatisfactoriness of pantheism and rejecting its conclusions as destructive, let us acknowledge the service which it has thus rendered, and the truth which it has helped to keep alive in the world. In its attitude to revelation, however, it was far more hostile to the supernatural principle than deism had been. Deism, indeed, by its recognition of a personal God, could never hold unwaveringly the incredibility of a miracle, and could with no consistency maintain that one was impossible. Pantheism was embarrassed by no such difficulties. Granting its assumption, a miracle was inconceivable. If there were no personal God, there could be no supernatural worker.

But how, then, are the facts of the Christian religion to be explained? How can we account for the early history of the Church, the influence which it has exerted, the form which it has assumed? The rationalistic theory, which admitted the general historical character of the

[1] Pfleiderer, p. 45.

facts, while denying the existence of any miraculous element in them, when applied to the whole life of Christ continuously, was speedily found wanting. And the clearest demonstration of its insufficiency came from the most powerful writer on the side of unbelief. Strauss's first "Life of Jesus" was published in 1835, only seven years later than that of Paulus,[1] and it was constructed on principles widely different from those of his predecessor. Strauss no longer acknowledged any certain historical element in the alleged facts of early Christian history. According to him, these "facts" were legends, fables, myths, embodying ideas which were then current in men's minds and which took bodily shape in these stories. How far any of the incidents recorded actually took place, the mythical school did not profess to know, — could not tell. There may be some nucleus of history within the record as it stands, but we cannot be sure how much of it is historical. We are, of course, quite sure that all the miraculous portion is fabulous, because a miracle is inconceivable and probably impossible.

But how, then, did these stories originate? They were, we are told, the product of the dreams and imaginations of the people among whom they arose, the embodiment of their

[1] But Paulus had published his "Commentary on the Gospels" twenty years before. He was much older than Strauss, having been born in 1761, while the latter was born in 1808.

Messianic expectations, the incarnation of their religious ideas.

When the first followers of Jesus had passed away,—this is the notion of Strauss,—then the popular imagination surrounded His memory with these miraculous incidents, which never indeed had any actual reality, but which they thought fitting to be associated with One who was the promised Messiah. The Jews expected Him to be of supernatural origin, hence the story of His miraculous conception. He must be greater than all the prophets who had preceded Him, and therefore greater wonders must be attributed to His ministry. Moses had fed the people with manna brought down from heaven; so He must make miraculous provision for the bodily wants of the multitude. Moses had turned the waters of the Nile into blood; a prophet greater than Moses must turn water into wine. Elijah had ascended to heaven in a chariot of fire; so Jesus must be received up in a cloud.

The theory was worked out with great elaboration and with unflinching consistency; and for a time it obtained an influence both extensive and profound. It dazzled men by its boldness; it fascinated them by the appearance of spirituality. Once grant its fundamental principle, and all difficulties were cleared up. But a delusion so gross could retain no permanent hold upon the minds of men. The inherent improbability of the theory became apparent almost before the shouts of triumph which greeted its promulgation had passed away.

It is enough here merely to glance[1] at the considerations which proved fatal to the mythical hypothesis. In the first place, the formation of a myth may be said to be a thing absolutely unknown in circumstances like those in which the Gospel stories are supposed to have arisen. There was not time for their origination in the manner asserted. Even if we bring down the dates of the four Gospels to the time assigned to them by Baur, — dates which are now generally abandoned and declared to be much too late by his followers, — even then we have the four universally accepted epistles of Saint Paul, written within a quarter of a century of the death of Jesus; and the notion of a series of myths like those of the Gospel story arising within a quarter of a century, or half a century, or even a much longer period, is too absurd to be entertained.

Besides, it is not true to say that the ideas prevalent among the Jews clothed themselves in the legendary forms of the Gospel narratives. The Jewish Messianic hopes[2] were, in many

---

[1] An examination of the application of the theory to the resurrection of Christ will be found in the eighth Lecture.

[2] These points have recently been brought out with great fulness by the Rev. V. H. Stanton, in his work on the Jewish Messiah.

respects, widely different from those which are embodied in the teaching of Jesus. It was the facts, the words and deeds of Jesus, which gave rise to the ideas; not the ideas which created the history. In addition to these defects, the mythical theory, in common with every attempt to destroy the supernatural character of the Gospel history, entirely failed to account for the unique and original personality of Jesus. None of these theories could account even for the idea of such a life; and how much less for its actual realization, and for the impression which it produced!

It is sufficient, for the present, thus to have indicated the causes of the weakness and of the ultimate and speedy failure of the mythical hypothesis. This, too, has had its day; and unbelief has had to seek out other weapons wherewith to assail the faith. Such, at least, is the lesson taught by the next kind of attack made upon the sacred Life. It was in 1863 that Renan published his "Vie de Jésus," which was followed almost immediately afterwards by the sketch (*Characterbild*) of Schenkel, and, in the following year, by Strauss's new "Life of Jesus for the German People."

The characteristics of these writings are full of instruction. As already mentioned, Renan had at first accepted, almost without question, the mythical hypothesis; but the influence of the soil of Palestine was too strong for him.

He tells us that he saw around him a fifth Gospel,[1] which made him feel that the events recorded in the other four were real occurrences. His book is of no great scientific importance, as it is founded upon no clear principle which receives consistent application throughout. It is merely a brilliant, sentimental romance, and therefore it has enjoyed an immense popularity; but it has hardly been taken seriously, and it has had little perceptible influence on theological opinion, unless we are to say that it induced Strauss to modify his theory, or at least to waver in his application of it, as is most certainly the case in his new attempt to write the sacred Life. And we think this honor, whatever its worth, cannot be denied to the brilliant French writer.

But it hardly needed the work of Renan to produce a different attitude towards the Scripture record. Among the proofs that the mythical theory was wearing out, and in the eyes of unbelievers becoming untenable, is the fact that Schenkel adopted almost simultaneously a line of thought very similar to that of Renan; for he, too, wavers between the rationalistic and the mythical positions, and his book, he tells us, was written before that of Renan was published. It was, in fact, clear that the mythical hypothesis could not be applied universally; but it was equally clear that the rationalistic

[1] Vie de Jésus (4th ed., Paris), Introd., p. liii.

theory had broken down. It only remained to adopt the one or the other, as either seemed best to suit the purpose for which it was employed. And this is precisely what Renan attempted. Thus, when he is accounting for the belief in the resurrection of Jesus, he advocates a theory somewhat similar to that of Strauss. It was, indeed, a modification of Strauss's earlier view, which was substantially adopted by the latter in his new "Life of Jesus."[1] It partakes both of the rationalistic and of the mythical character, without being wholly referable to either theory.

It was different with other miracles,—with the raising of Lazarus, for example. Here Renan was not embarrassed by the difficulties which forbid the application of the rationalistic hypothesis, pure and simple, to the resurrection of Jesus, as had been done by Paulus. At the grave of Lazarus he is a simple rationalist. According to his view, something like the raising of a dead man did take place at Bethany. But it was a scene got up by Jesus and Lazarus, in order to impress His enemies, and perhaps put a stop to their machinations, as they were now beginning to plot against His life.

Strauss himself takes very nearly the same ground in his new "Life" (1864). In this work, he says, he makes more use of conscious imposture. In his earlier book the myths were

---

[1] This theory will be considered in the eighth Lecture.

represented as having grown up spontaneously, and clustered around the slender thread of true history, which was quite hidden by them. But the world had begun to deride and to discard this explanation, the theologians of all schools had gradually come to pronounce it untenable, and Strauss himself, while preferring to retain it as a general working theory, found himself under the necessity of stopping some of the rents in his garment with the old patches of rationalism. It was tolerably clear that certain parts of the Gospel story could not have grown up spontaneously. Still it was impossible for him to admit any supernatural explanation of their origin; and therefore it became necessary to fall back upon the clumsy devices of rationalism and its theories of deception which he had, at a former period, helped to explode. And this is science! This is the work of men who tell us that we must have no presuppositions, no assumptions, — that we must come to the examination of facts without prejudice, and with the simple desire to discover the truth!

III. It was eight years after the publication of his new "Life" that Strauss put forth his last work, "The Old Faith and the New."[1] He was now sixty-four years of age, and his course was nearly run. He died in the following year (1873). He tells us that he hears a voice within him, bidding him give an account of his stew-

---

[1] Der alte und der neue Glaube (1872).

ardship, and this is his response. His belief is materialistic atheism; his religion is the worship of the universe; his hope is the grave. In a pamphlet written near the time at which he published his new "Life of Jesus," he says that he has never yielded to the temptation of deceiving himself by borrowing from another world. It could hardly be otherwise; those who do not believe in a personal God can have no ground for belief in a future life.

It has been said that the last utterances of Strauss show a considerably widened interval[1] between his point of view and that of Christian faith; but it must be admitted that such a criticism is true only of the form of his belief, and not of its substance. In his earlier works he certainly retained the name of Christian, and this he entirely abandoned at last. But there was little left to surrender. This will be evident if we compare his earlier with his later utterances. In his treatise on "The Transient and Permanent in Christianity,"[2] published soon after his first "Life of Jesus," he remarks that "Christ must remain for us the highest that we know in relation to religion, as that one without whose presence in the mind no perfect piety is possible." In one of his books on Ulrich

---

[1] Even Zeller indicates this difference in his "Sketch of Strauss," § 51 (Bonn, 1874).

[2] Vergängliches und Bleibendes in Christenthum (1836 or 1837).

Hutten[1] he says : "Why should it not be acknowledged on both sides that we now find in the Biblical history only poetry and truth [*Dichtung und Wahrheit*, referring to the title of Goethe's autobiography], and in the ecclesiastical dogmas only significant symbols ; but that we must yield unaltered respect to the moral contents of Christianity, and to the character of its Founder, so far as His human form is yet to be recognized under the incrustation of miracles in which the first historians of his life have enclosed him?"

His tone in "The Old Faith and the New" is quite different. It can hardly be said, however, that his principles are radically changed, although, in his "Confession," to the question, "Are we still Christians?" he answers flatly, "No." For the Christianity which he formerly professed was a religion which ignored all the fundamental doctrines of the Gospel, and the supernatural origin, character, and work of our Lord, and which resolved all the facts which we regard as historical into mere ideas or notions; and he believed then, no more than in his later period, in a God whom he could worship, who could hear and answer his prayer, and with whom he could hold living communion. In short, his teaching was, in all its phases, essentially, if not always formally, atheistic. For if that which we call God and the world are iden-

[1] Translation of the Gespräche (1860).

tical, or if God is a mere *Anima mundi*, without self-consciousness, without intelligence, without will, then in the proper sense of the word there is no God, and so no soul and no immortality. At first Dr. Strauss was implicitly atheistical; at the last he is so explicitly.

And this may be said to be the last word of unbelief, its final testimony or confession.[1] It has run its course, it has passed through its varying phases,—theological, metaphysical, positive; deistic, pantheistic, atheistic,—and this is its last word, its only remaining word. Rationalistic deism has said its say, and is dead; the mythical theory with its hazy pantheism has gone the same way; and now we are confronted by a dull and dogged atheism which does not profess[2] to account for the origin of the Gospel and the Church, but is only sure that they do not come from God, simply because there is no God for them to come from.

To some it may appear that this is, for the Christian faith, far from being a hopeful state of matters. If we hold a different opinion, it is from no wish to adopt the point of view of a thoughtless optimism, but from a calm review of history and a dispassionate consideration of the nature and needs of man.

[1] Strauss calls "Der alte und der neue Glaube," *ein Bekenntniss*, a confession.
[2] This is denied. We shall see, however, in subsequent lectures, what value can be attached to the explanations offered.

The Church of Christ exists, and her existence and her history and her influence must be accounted for. Christian civilization exists, and must be explained as to its sources and its progress in the world. Humanity exists, with all its wants to be supplied, with all its many questions to be answered, with a heart which cries out for the living God, and which will need many powerful arguments before it can be brought to believe that there is no God. Man does not willingly despair; at least he cannot easily acquiesce in a philosophy of despair. "Hope springs eternal in the human breast;" but this is because there is in the human breast an ineradicable sense of God. And therefore we do not believe that man will ever abandon the desire to know God, and to know the nature and meaning of that Gospel which professes supremely to be a message from Him.[1]

Here is our hope for the future. Men will not and cannot abstain from questions concerning God, duty, immortality. We are contented if they will go on asking and if they will hear the answers which are given to their questions. No wise advocate of Christian Revelation expects or desires a blind and unreflecting acquiescence in his teaching. What we want is the most searching examination into the truth of our testimony, in order to the attainment of a reasonable and well-grounded faith. We have

[1] See Note B.

not followed fables, either cunningly devised or spontaneously developed ; and even if we believed the prospects of the Church to be darker than ever they were, as we believe them to be brighter than they have been for many a day, we should remember the words which comforted the most heroic of Germans, and one of the greatest of men: " God is in the midst of her, therefore she shall not be removed: God shall help her, and that right early."

LECTURE II.

CIVILIZATION AND CHRISTIANITY.

The Gospel in the World. — Christian Ideal and Christian Life contrasted. — Has Christianity failed? — Modern Civilization and Christianity. — Opposing Views. — I. The World before Christ: Claims of the Ancient World real; Serious Defects; vitiated by Egoism. — Plato and Aristotle. — Citizens, Slaves, Barbarians, Enemies. — Greeks and Romans alike. — Cicero. — Condition of various Classes: 1. Women, — Status, Marriage, Dependence; 2. Working Classes, — Manual Labor thought degrading; 3. Slaves, — Slavery accepted by the Philosophers, the Laws relating to Slavery, Slavery in Practice, Exceptions, Doctrine of Stoics. — II. The Need supplied: the Gospel of Human Brotherhood; its Foundation in Christ. — The Kingdom of God; its Subjects; its Laws. — Changes effected: 1. Condition of Women; 2. Laboring Classes; 3. The Poor, — provided for by Christianity; the Emperor Julian; 4. Slaves, — Objection that there is no Christian Command for Emancipation; Answer, — what the Gospel has done, what it has to do; 5. War; 6. Legislation. — Conclusion.

WHAT has the Gospel of Jesus Christ accomplished for the world? It is a fair question. Even if we were warned that the truth would certainly meet with opposition, even if the very nature of the message carried within itself the prophecy of conflict, we are still bound to believe, we have been taught to believe, that the propagation of the Gospel throughout the world could not be without great and lasting and far-reaching effects. Jesus Christ is the true King of men. He, when He is lifted up, is appointed to draw all men unto Him. The heathen have been given to Him as an heritage, and the utmost ends of the earth for a possession.

No one can maintain that the Gospel has been without effect. Throughout the whole of what we call the civilized world, it has supplanted the ancient faiths of heathendom and has become the dominant religion. Nearly all civilized nations call themselves Christian. Under the shadow of the Cross no other faith can be said to flourish. In nearly all the places where prayer is wont to be made, it is in the Name of Jesus that all men bow, and that Name is accounted to be above all other names. So much may be confidently alleged by the disciple of Christ, and the unbeliever cannot gainsay it.

It is evident, however, that the mere profession of Christianity, important as it is, cannot be regarded as a complete answer to the question : What has the Gospel, what has Christ, done for mankind ? Not every one that calls Him Lord will have a right to a place in His Kingdom. It is not enough to be hearers of His word. This is nothing, perhaps worse than nothing, unless we are also doers of it. In short, it is the participation in the spirit of Christ which constitutes and evinces a true and living relation between Himself and His professed followers. And it is this conformity of men to the mind and character of Christ which alone can be accepted as satisfactory evidence that the Gospel has worked in the world those beneficial results which it claims to have the power to produce.

Every one can see that we are here entering upon an inquiry more difficult than we were at first prepared for. Not only is it almost impossible to determine the true quality of human actions, conduct, character; but we must be prepared for the attempt which will be made by our adversaries to establish a violent contrast between the ideal of the Gospel and the real of actual Christian life. It is easy enough to show that such a contrast exists.[1] Whether we take the character and life of Jesus Christ Himself, or the ideal which He prescribes, or the commands and precepts by which He requires that we shall be guided, we cannot deny that the ordinary life of professing Christians falls far short of His example and His rule. Men as a whole, — the men who are living around us, — could not be accurately described as Christlike. Nay, further, such a description would not apply with any amount of exactness to the inner circle of those who seem to be making

---

[1] Since these lines were written, the writer has seen Mr. Cotter Morison's "Service of Man" (see Notes B, E, and G). Mr. Morison gives many proofs of the prevalence of moral evil during the Christian period; but he takes little notice of what Christianity has actually effected.

a more strenuous endeavor than most other men, to follow in the footsteps of Jesus Christ.

What inference shall we deduce from these admitted facts ? Shall we allow that the enemies of the Cross have a right to say that the Gospel has been a failure ? Supposing that we had no interest in the decision of the question, is this the answer which we should judge to be a true one ? Certainly not ; and this for various reasons. In the first place, we never expect, and we have no right to expect, the real to correspond exactly with the ideal. It is a great matter if men really do hold fast the ideal, if in any measure they keep it before their eyes and strive towards its realization. And this, at least, may be said for Christian society, — it has before it a higher ideal of character, aim, duty, than has ever been known outside the boundaries of Christendom.[1]

And then there are other questions that would have to be answered. For example, this question : Not merely are men now made perfect by the doctrines and influences of Christianity; but are they better or worse than they were without the Gospel ? Are Christian countries better than countries which are not Christian ? Are those Christian countries better or worse

---

[1] The objection that Christians are worse than their creed is surely a strong argument in behalf of the Gospel. What a poor system would that be which lowered its ideal and rule of life to the level of the life of its adherents !

in which the Christianity is most like the Christianity of the Bible, and in which the sacred volume has freest course? Are the Christian portions of the world better since they became Christian than they were when they were heathen, or are they worse? Do the best men among us attribute the good in themselves to the word and the power of Christ, or not?

Now, some of these questions may be answered with at least an approximation to certainty; and if they can be answered in the affirmative, then the verdict must be given in favor of Christianity. It is something of this kind that we are now to attempt. We propose to show that what we call modern civilization, in its prevailing ideas and sentiments, in its beneficent legislation, in its general spirit of mercy and compassion, is the creation of Christianity; that it is infinitely superior to the civilization of pre-Christian times, differing from that not merely in degree but in kind, and that we have therefore in this very civilization a standing evidence of the beneficial effects of the Gospel.

Before advancing to the particular proofs of these assertions, we must not ignore the theories which have been advanced in opposition to that which we maintain. For instance, it has been held by one school,[1] that religion, and more particularly Christianity, has been so far from

[1] Dr. Draper may be mentioned as a leading representative of this class.

favoring the progress of the higher civilization that it has been a positive hindrance to it ; and a contrast has, in this respect, been drawn between the narrowing and depressing influences of the Reformation as compared with the genial and liberalizing tendencies of the classical Renaissance. On the other hand, it has been admitted that religion and civilization have gone hand in hand ; but it has been represented [1] that the religious beliefs of an age have been the outcome of the civilization of the age rather than the principal influence by which it was moulded.

To those who possess an intimate acquaintance with the movement known as the Renaissance, little need be said as to its power to put new life into human society. But the best answer to this and other theories, the best evidence that the higher principles and the nobler elements of modern civilization are the outcome of Christianity, will be found in a simple consideration of historical facts. When we recall the true character of the heathen civilization of Greece and Rome, when we consider the principles of the Gospel of Christ, and when we further contemplate the actual civilization of the world in the midst of which we are living, we shall then be able to say how far mankind has been raised and ennobled by the Gospel, and whether that

---

[1] This is the general view of Mr. Buckle in his "History of Civilization."

Gospel was the mere development of principles already working in the world, or was a new life and a new spirit brought into the bosom of humanity by the revelation of God.

I. It is hardly needful to say that such an attempt involves no disrespect to the earlier ages of the world, no effort to misrepresent anything that was good or true or beautiful in their achievements, no failure to render homage to the great minds which they produced. Rather, from our own point of view, shall we often wonder that they did so much, and that, in their gropings after truth, they did not go astray more widely from the absolute rule of truth and righteousness.

The true, the beautiful, and the good, — these were the three watchwords of the thinkers of ancient Greece; and upon these all true human development, culture, and civilization must ultimately depend. The intellectual or speculative, the æsthetic, and the moral principles are all of importance; but the last is the greatest of the three. Perhaps the sentiment of the beautiful has never been more exquisitely embodied than in the literature and art of Greece. And if we cannot place their attainment of the truth on the same level with their realization of the beautiful, there has, perhaps, seldom been manifested a more ardent devotion to its pursuit than was found among the nobler intellects of this great people. It is when we contemplate their notions of the *good* that we see how far they fell short of the Christian idea. What is the notion which now, by universal consent, we place in the foremost rank of human qualities? What is the principle out of which we develop all other virtues and graces and excellences? It is the principle of love, benevolence, unselfishness, — call it by what name you please, — the principle by which we recognize that all other men have the same rights and privileges as ourselves, — the principle which bids each man do unto another as he would have that other do unto himself. That principle was utterly unknown, as a fundamental virtue, by heathen antiquity.[1]

When Plato[2] laid down the four cardinal virtues of Wisdom, Courage, Temperance, Justice, he found no place in his scheme for love, or for the humility and self-sacrifice which are its necessary attendants. And although it might seem that in Plato and in Aristotle, and more particularly in the former, the individual was subordinated to the community by the idea of the State, a deeper consideration of the subject will show that the selfish principle was strengthened rather than weakened by this idea. It is true, indeed, that, in Plato's view, the moral life in a well-ordered State was the highest conceivable moral-

---

[1] I am under obligations, in this lecture, to some sermons of Adolphe Monod, published after his death, and still more to a lecture by Dr. Mangold, of Bonn.

[2] Republic, book iv. (ed. Baiter, vol. xiii. pp. 113 ss.).

ity, and that in the ancient State every citizen was bound to sacrifice himself, if necessary, to lay down his life, for the good of the community, and thus it might seem that individualism and selfishness were condemned; yet it must be remembered, on the other side, that everything which the citizen expended for the State he received back again with interest. The Grecian State, and it was the same with the Roman, recognized the citizen alone as having any civil rights or privileges. All other members of the human race were regarded, if foreigners, as barbarians or enemies; if dwelling within the borders of the State, as in a state of pupillage, dependence, or servitude, as having no claim to any civil privileges which belonged to the citizens alone. Thus a system which seemed likely to destroy selfishness and build up a religion of humanity, turns out to be merely constitutive of a privileged and limited aristocracy; all who are outside this privileged class are regarded as hardly belonging to the same order in creation.

In this respect Greeks and Romans were alike. In their view a foreigner was a barbarian and an enemy, to whom no participation in human rights was to be allowed. Even Plato[1] and Aristotle — the noblest representatives of Greek thought, and the pioneers of the philosophy of the world — had no other judgment to pronounce

[1] Republic, book v. (ed. Baiter, vol. xiii. pp. 156 ss.). Aristotle, Politics, i. 2.

on the position of foreigners; and Cicero,[1] the mouthpiece of Roman society, echoes their sentiment, declaring that barbarians might, without scruple, be killed, and sold as slaves. And in this matter they were not mere promulgators of a theory which, like many parts of the "Republic" of Plato, was hardly regarded as capable of realization; as a matter of fact, barbarians taken in war were sold as slaves, and compelled to engage in the gladiatorial conflicts, in which multitudes were slain for the amusement of the people in Rome.

But it was not merely towards foreign barbarians that this cynical disregard for all men who were outside the sacred boundaries of citizenship was manifested. Whole classes of their own people, among Greeks and Romans alike, were refused the recognition of any privileges save those which their masters might concede to them, not as rights, but as acts of charity.

1. Among these we might mention, first, as being in our own view the most grievous, the condition of *women* among the ancients. Aristotle,[2] indeed, commends the Greeks for not placing their women on a level with slaves, as is done by the Eastern nations; but the rank assigned to them was of the lowest. Thus we find Socrates[3] asking his disciple Critobulus with

[1] De Officiis, i. 12; iii. 11.
[2] Politics, i. 2.
[3] Xenophon, Economics, c. 3, § 12.

whom he would rather not converse than with his wife, and the disciple immediately answering, "No one." Any intellectual or moral fellowship between man and wife was made impossible by the subordinate position assigned to the latter. The wife, in this system of things, was merely regarded as the mother of future citizens and the manager of the household, — in short, as a kind of servant to her husband. So long as the chief virtues of the married woman were comprised in the words of the Roman epitaph, "She sat in her house and span wool,"[1] her place of subjection was inevitable. And this was fully recognized in the laws and traditions of the country.

The oldest form of Roman marriage was the purchase of a wife. The daughter passed, like a household chattel, from the hands of her father to those of her husband. She never had any idea of independence; and after the death of her husband she came under the protection of his relatives. Indeed, so completely was a wife regarded as the mere property of her husband, that he might transfer her to another man; and we find Cato the elder leaving his wife to his friend Hortensius. In the later period of the Emperors, while the condition of wives seemed to be improved, it was in fact much worse. They were then regarded, indeed, as possessing a measure of independence; but, unaccustomed

---

[1] Corpus Inscriptionum Latinarum, vol. i. no. 1,007.

as they were to a sense of their own dignity, they turned this new-found liberty to licentiousness, abandoning themselves to senseless luxury, to shameless libertinage, — making amends, as it were, for the long oppression of their sex. Doubtless there were brilliant exceptions in every age; but the brightness with which they shine out on the page of Roman history reveals the darkness by which they were surrounded.

2. What, again, was the condition of the *artisan* and the *trading classes* in this state of things? One of the fundamental ideas of modern civilization, that every honorable kind of labor ennobles a man, was unknown to the heathen world. To those who were employed in any kind of manual labor the highest rights of humanity could not be conceded, because they were engaged in the daily struggle for the necessaries of life, and so were unable to give their whole powers to the service of the State. They were regarded as in a sense the slaves of the public, and as slaves they were held incapable of any real elevation of mind. It is in the most matter-of-course manner that Plato and Aristotle declare that true virtue is not to be expected of those who have to work, — at the most only the servile virtue of obedience; and Plato adds that it is, after all, a matter of indifference whether a manual laborer live a virtuous or a vicious life, as it is only the virtue of the ruling and law-giving classes that is a matter of importance.

Can the workman, then, be regarded as a man, as a human being?[1] But how did it fare with him when he was sick and miserable and dependent upon foreign aid? It was well for him when he could find a place of shelter and protection; he had no claim upon the State; and whether he lived or died, society would acknowledge no duty to hold out to him a helping hand.[2]

3. But there was a class with whom it fared worse than with the laborer, — the *slaves*. The institution of slavery, with all its attendant evils, had been so familiar to the people that even the philosophers had come to look upon it as an ordinance of Nature. It appeared to them that two quite different classes of men were brought into the world, — the one qualified for the enjoyment of liberty; the other actually disqualified for this privilege, and thereby condemned to bondage. These men had no claim to be recognized as among the privileged classes.[3] Hence it is that Varro,[4] in his work on agriculture, expressly classes the slaves along with beasts of burden, but only, from their having the gift of speech, as capable of a higher kind of service; and even Cicero,[5] in writing to his friend Atticus,

---

[1] Aristotle, Politics, iii. 4; viii. 2; vii. 9. Plato, Republic, book iv. (ed. Baiter, vol. xiii. p. 104).

[2] Plautus, Trinummus, Act ii. Sc. 2, vv. 58, 59.

[3] Plato, Laws, vi. (ed. Baiter, vol. xiv. p. 186). Aristotle, Politics, i. 3–6.

[4] De re rustica, i. 17.   [5] Ad Atticum, i. 12.

thinks he is bound to offer some excuse because of his excessive grief at the death of his slave Sositheus.

And this theory of the philosophers was embodied in the laws of the country. Roman law declared the slave to be the entire property of his master, a thing which could be dealt with in the same manner as any other piece of property; and it offered to the slave no protection of any kind. Husband and wife might be separated, children sold away from their parents, the slave might be maimed or put to death by his master, without the restraint of any penalty to follow. And the legal condition of the slave was in no degree ameliorated in practice. In the early days of Greece and Rome it seems to have been different. To the simple tiller of the ground the slave was a kind of companion or partner in work. But in the later days of Roman greatness the state of things was altered. The number of slaves had increased immensely throughout the Empire; and the sternest measures became necessary in order to keep them in a state of subjection. Consequently they were treated with the greatest severity. The owners were not all equally harsh. Few, probably, rose to the height of inhumanity mentioned by Juvenal as having been shown by a Roman master when he was entreated to spare an innocent slave whom he had condemned to death. "What!" was the reply, "do you consider a slave to be a human being? Be he innocent or not, this is my will and my command. My will is law."[1] Probably, also, there were not many women so inhuman as those who, accustomed to the bloody sights of the circus, made their female slaves wait upon them naked to the waist, and punished them for any misconduct or mistake by pricking them with a bodkin or a needle until the blood came; and yet there were cases in which old and worn-out slaves were driven from their home and left to die of hunger and nakedness by the wayside.[2]

It is quite true that some men, here and there in this ancient society, gained glimpses of higher truths which contained within them prophecies of emancipation and liberty. But what was the real effect of these guesses and gropings after the knowledge of God and man? Some there were who found their way to a perception of the unity of God, and taught that all men, as His creatures, were alike manifestations of the Divine, and were bound to recognize each other as such. But there was no foundation for the doctrine but the speculations of philosophers, and it seemed to men in general as a dream, and it passed away like a cloud which hardly let fall a drop of dew upon the earth to slake its thirst.

The stoics [3] might protest against the current

---

[1] Satire, vi. vv. 222 ss.
[2] Plutarch, Lives, vol. ii. Cicero, Cato Major, c. 4, 5.
[3] Seneca, De Beneficiis, iii. 18–28.

notions of liberty and bondage; might declare that the man who was in bondage to his passions was the real slave, while he who was kept in bondage by his fellow-man and yet was possessed of wisdom, was indeed the free man. But such doctrines, however they might raise and comfort the individual, made no difference in the general condition of slaves.

Seneca, one of the noblest representatives of the great stoic school, could declare that "Man should be a sacred thing to man;"[1] but the words passed unheeded, or if they extorted a momentary tribute of admiration or of acquiescence, they had no practical significance and led to no results. Something more was needed than such occasional testimonies, — something that rested on deeper foundations and was commended by more powerful sanctions.

II. That *Something*, which the heathen philosopher longed for, which should bring home to men a sense of their brotherhood, was even then in the midst of that degraded Roman society, although for the most part they knew it not. A contemporary of Seneca, the converted Jew, Saul of Tarsus, Paul the apostle of Jesus Christ, was declaring to all who would hear him the Gospel of human brotherhood, not for Greek or for Roman or for Jew only, but for the whole human race, — a doctrine which was destined to

[1] "Homo sacra res homini." — Seneca, Ep. 93. 33.

throw down the barriers which separated man from man and class from class, and to declare that there were no real privileges and blessings known upon earth which were not open to the whole family of man.

But upon what foundation could this new truth be made to rest? And how could it be hoped that it would find free course among a race so little prepared for its reception? The answer to the question is found in the manifestation and in the work of Jesus Christ here upon .earth.

What was He in His own person? He was God manifest in the flesh. The Eternal Word, one with the Father, had taken into indissoluble union with Himself the nature of man, — not of this man or of that man, not the nature of any privileged nation or family, but the nature of our common humanity. Here was the greatest privilege, the privilege of union with God accorded to mankind. There is nothing higher to which men can attain, and there is no one who cannot attain to it. Here at one blow is shattered the Old World selfishness which doomed the larger portion of mankind to a state of dependence and bondage. Men are brethren, and as such cannot be regarded as essentially different in their nature and capacities.

As a consequence of this first manifestation, which received its full meaning in the life and work and sacrifice and death and resurrection of the God-man, there was proclaimed a Kingdom of God upon the earth, over which the Deliverer was appointed to reign, and into which all men were to be admitted as subjects. And the idea of the Kingdom was in a large measure realized on the very day of its inauguration. On that first Christian Pentecost, men from all parts of the world heard the glad message, and pressed into the Kingdom of light and liberty, and became brethren in the family of God. No question was there of wealth or poverty, of freedom or bondage; whosoever believed and was baptized, entered into the sacred fellowship of the Church.

Let it be granted that there was a moment's doubt as to the method in which those privileges were to be extended to all the nations of the earth. God does not ever seem to lead men into complete and perfect truth all at once. And yet there was no doubt among the Apostles, as to whether others than the children of Abraham should participate in the blessings of the Covenant. The only question was as to the necessity of their first becoming Jewish proselytes. And this question was soon set at rest, practically, under Divine guidance, by Saint Peter, and in a more systematic and reasoned manner by Saint Paul, appointed to be specially the Apostle of the Gentiles. Then did the whole truth which was involved in the Incarnation shine forth upon the Church. Then did it become self-evident that in Christ Jesus there is neither Jew nor Greek, neither bond nor free, neither male nor female.

And if this were the constitution of the Kingdom, the nature of the principles of the Kingdom followed as a necessary consequence. The law of the Kingdom of God was love, — love to the Father, love to the Great Elder Brother, and in Him love to all the Brethren. And herein is the greatness of the Law of the Gospel demonstrated, as compared with all the feeble and powerless human systems of ethics which had attempted to regulate the life and conduct of men in the past. It carried its principle, its argument, its proof within itself. It sprang out of the relations established by the manifestation of God in Christ, and by the grafting of the members into His mystical Body. Nor was this all. It was enforced and made an actual inner power by the gift of the Holy Spirit of Love. God could now dwell upon the earth with men, since man was now ascended into heaven and seated at the right hand of God. The law of love is no longer a mere theory however beautiful, a mere precept however binding; it is a power, the very power of God working in the heart of man. Such is, at least, the claim of the Gospel and of the Church of Jesus Christ. And to this extent, at least, its pretensions must be conceded; this is its message to the children of men, however it may be received, or whatever may be its effects. Man is the child of God. The lost child he is when he is living in ignorance and in sin; but in Jesus Christ the lost child found and brought back to his Father's house. Nor need we fear the test of facts, when we declare that this new doctrine did not remain a mere theory, — that it became a power, a fact in human society; so that men were "no longer strangers and sojourners, but fellow-citizens with the saints, and of the household of God;"[1] and this changed relation worked a revolution among all the down-trodden classes of human society. Let us note the change which passed more particularly upon those classes of whose condition under heathenism we have already spoken.

1. *Woman* was placed on a level with man in the Kingdom of God. There was no longer a distinction of male and female. It was, therefore, no longer possible to assign to her a servile position in the family and in the social system. And hence the Christian Apostle says to Christian husbands, "Love your wives," and finds in marriage a type of the union of Christ with the Church. And from that time marriage assumed a new significance, and the wife became the partner and companion of the husband, and the gentle ruler of the household. As a consequence, the character of the Christian woman became ennobled, and invested with a dignity which even the heathen could not

[1] Eph. ii. 19.

ignore; so that an opponent of Christianity, like the heathen rhetorician Libanius, was constrained to exclaim, "What wives those Christians have!"

2. How, again, could the *laboring classes* fail to receive a regenerating influence from the Gospel, when Jesus Himself had been a working-man, a carpenter; when His first followers and the propagators of His Gospel had been fishermen, His greatest Apostle a tent-maker who made it his boast that he preached the Gospel without charge to his hearers because he could maintain himself, working with his own hands? Thus were labor and the condition of the laborer made honorable in the Church, since the laborer was a child of God, and, whether capable of earthly citizenship or not, a citizen in the Kingdom of God, having full right to the brotherly love of the Divine Family. And so it came to pass that the mind of the Middle Ages, which counted prayer the highest service of man, could say, "To labor is to pray;" and so it is that we can now regard work in the truest sense as worship.

3. To none, perhaps, was the change produced by the message of Christ more significant and more profound than to the *poor*. It was one of the notes of the Kingdom of Heaven, indicated specially by our Lord Himself, that "the poor have the Gospel preached to them."[1]

[1] Matt. xi. 5.

In the Church of Christ the poor man found a community which recognized in him a child of God, and accorded to him, without reserve, all the privileges of citizens in the Kingdom of God. He found brethren who not only greeted him with a loving welcome, but also helped to supply his needs out of the weekly offerings presented every Lord's Day at their gathering together for Eucharist and for worship. Now, for the first time in the history of the world, arose houses of refuge and shelter for the poor, the needy, the infirm. The Romans had hospitals for their soldiers; they had no public provision for the sick and needy among the poor. Even the heathen could not help being struck by this new and strange development of humanity in the Church. Julian the Apostate, — one of the bitterest, if also one of the noblest, of the enemies of the Nazarene, — who professed an ardent belief in the glory of the old paganism, which he labored so eagerly to restore, and for that purpose waged a war of annihilation against the Church in the fourth century, yet could not withhold his admiration from the Christians in their care for the poor of the flock. It was in vain that he endeavored to awaken the same spirit in the adherents of the old religion. He writes, in his disappointment, to Arsacius, the Archpriest of Galatia: " Hellenism does not prosper as we could wish, and this through the fault of its adherents. For they are destitute of the virtues of the despised Galileans; and whilst among the despicable people of the Jews there is none who is allowed to beg, the Christians not only support their own poor, but contribute to the relief of some of ours also, whom we leave, without assistance, to their tender care."[1] What this has grown to, no one living in these lands needs to be told. For every species and form of human suffering merciful provision is made in our almshouses, our infirmaries, our hospitals; because the Spirit of Jesus Christ, the spirit of human brotherhood, has penetrated our society, and leavened many hearts which know not even whence that new spirit has come, some even which yield no conscious homage to that Great Elder Brother who has brought us this new grace from our Father in heaven.

4. We have spoken of the condition of *slaves* in the heathen world; and it has been made a reproach to the Gospel of Christ that it contains no command for the emancipation of the slaves, and that every Christian nation has exercised the same tyranny over bondsmen which was common in the ancient world. Nay, more, it is argued that Christianity has actually been a support of slavery, since Saint Paul sent back to Philemon his runaway slave Onesimus, as though he had a right to claim him as his property.

[1] Julian, Epistle 49.

There is really no considerable difficulty in meeting these objections, if men are only willing to receive the answer.

Let it be remarked, in the first place, that Christianity was not a code of laws and precepts, but a principle. To have reduced the principle of love to God and love to man to a series of special commands would have been to narrow and cramp its sphere and influence throughout all ages. No set of precepts, however large and varied, can include every case and every variety of circumstances which may arise in the development of human society; while the principles of the Gospel are so living, so expansive, so flexible, that no conceivable condition or circumstances of man or of society can escape their application and their force. Christ refused to be a divider or to interfere in particular cases between man and man which the individual conscience could decide; and we can see that this was the way in which alone a noble and a spiritual morality could be made possible.

With regard to the particular institution of slavery, it was, humanly speaking, impossible for the Church to command its abolition. It would have been to embarrass itself with undertakings which would have hindered, perhaps rendered utterly ineffectual, its own proper work. Are we, moreover, certain that the immediate emancipation of the servile classes would have been a gain, we say not to the owners but to the bondsmen themselves? There are some men, by no means irrational, inhumane, or unchristian, who wish that, in more places than one, the liberation of the slave might have been more gradual.

But, however all this may be, — and it is unnecessary to offer here any opinion on these subjects, — it is tolerably clear to all who give unprejudiced consideration to the subject, that the truth and the power which have emancipated the slave in every land, had their origin in the Gospel of Jesus Christ. That was the first teacher of our common origin, common powers and capacities, common rights and privileges. It is in Jesus Christ, not in Plato or in Seneca or in Moses, that there is neither Jew nor Gentile, neither Greek nor Barbarian, neither bond nor free. When we learn that God hath made of one blood all nations of men for to dwell upon the face of the earth, — when we know that Jesus Christ tasted death for every man, died for the sins of the whole world, — then we know that slavery and every kind of oppression is doomed. Not all at once do we perceive the full meaning which is contained in our brotherhood in Jesus Christ. Light breaks slowly through the darkness of earth, dispelling gradually our ignorance, our prejudices, our selfishness; but when the darkness is gone and the true light shineth upon us, then do we see that its full glory is derived from that Sun of righteousness which has risen with healing in its beams, — that it comes from Him who is the Light of the World, whom following we shall never walk in darkness.

5. It is true that the Gospel of Jesus Christ has not yet had free course. We still see, alas! the remains of the old selfish individualism in the relations of peoples to peoples, and of men to men; and yet how vast the change which has already been effected! It is true that *wars* have not ceased to the ends of the earth. We have not yet broken every bow and cut every spear in sunder. But even here the spirit of the Gospel is manifested. Nations do not rush into war with the impetuosity of wild beasts, eager for the fray and thirsting for blood. Even when there is no reasonable pretext for hostilities, those who begin the warfare must convince themselves that there is a cause, must put forth some plausible plea to the civilized world as a reason for their having recourse to the sword; and when wars do break out, and the weakest has to yield, the conqueror no longer dares — may we not say, no longer desires — to ravage the conquered soil with fire and sword. Among many other proofs of the changed conditions of warfare, may we not mention with gratitude to God, that, after the close of the great civil war in this country, not one person was put to death for participation in the rebellion?

6. And what shall we say of the internal affairs of nations, — of our government, our *legislation*, the actual administration of justice? Has it not come to this, that no nation in which the Gospel of Christ has free course can now, for any length of time, be governed otherwise than for the good of the community at large? No prestige, no lengthened possession of the place of authority, however far back it may reach into the past, no halo of glory and dignity which may rest upon the brow of the ruler, will retain him in his seat if his rule is tyrannical and injurious to his subjects. Wisdom may now say with fresh emphasis, " By me kings rule and princes decree justice."

And what of our legislation? Is it not inspired by a pure spirit of benevolence, so that no law could even be proposed or thought of unless it could plead its tendency to ameliorate the condition of the people? Mistakes enough are doubtless made in legislation as in everything else, for we are not infallible; but here as elsewhere breathes the spirit of Christ, — the spirit of loving brotherhood which will not suffer the poor and the weak to be trodden underfoot, but cultivates mercy, kindness, generosity to all who need.

It is always easy to point out faults and sins and shortcomings; and in our modern civilization there are not wanting features and tendencies which are at variance with the principles of truth and justice and mercy. Yet they are not the characteristic marks of that order of things to which it is our privilege to belong. They are violations of its spirit, exceptions to its general tendency, spots and blots upon its fair face. And we are not cherishing unwarranted hopes and expectations when we look forward to the time when they shall have disappeared. That time is coming

> "When man to man the world o'er
> Shall brothers be for all that."

And this hope we cherish not merely because the thing itself is desirable, and is now universally acknowledged to be desirable, but because we have seen a principle in operation in the world which has already vindicated its claim to humanize[1] mankind and diffuse the principle of brotherly love among them; because we now behold this principle going forth throughout the human race conquering and to conquer, and we behold alike in the inner power and vitality of the principle itself, and in the mighty and enduring conquests which it has already achieved, the sure pledge, the promise which only awaits the appointed time of its fulfilment, that as there is but one God and one Lord, one Father of whom the whole Family in heaven and earth is named, so there will be, in His good

[1] See Note C.

time, but one Family,— one in truth, in love, in sympathy, — gathered around His throne, acknowledging themselves as brethren, knit together in one communion and fellowship in the mystical Body of Christ.

LECTURE III.

PERSONAL CULTURE AND RELIGION.

Man, Individual and Social. — Transition from Civilization to personal Culture. — Man's Nature and Culture. — Points of Agreement. — I. Theories of Culture various, but reducible to two, Religious and Non-Religious: 1. The Non-Religious, — (1) Social, (2) Scientific, (3) Literary, (4) Positivist; 2. The Christian. — II. Means of Attainment: Human Culture not undervalued, but insufficient, as not taking account of Man's whole Nature; illustrated: 1. Idea of Immortality; 2. Responsibility, — (1) Conscience, (2) the Idea of God, (3) Consciousness of Sin, (4) how met by the Gospel, (5) Effects produced. — Mill. — Goethe and Saint François de Sales. — Luther and Rousseau. — General Effects. — The Christian Ideal. — Lecky. — Mill on Belief in Immortality; on the Life and Teaching of Jesus.

WE may study the nature of man in two different ways. We may select the individual as a specimen of the race, and see in him all the powers, capacities, tendencies which are manifested on a larger scale in the whole human family. Or we may begin at the other end of the scale. We may study the race of man as a whole, in society, in nationalities, in the wide extent and lengthened progress of human history, and learn from such an investigation all the wonderful possibilities which are contained within the individual man.

Both of these methods of inquiry have been pursued with more or less of success. But neither of them, by itself, will conduct us to the knowledge of the whole truth concerning our own nature. A mere system of individualism which ignores the corporate character of the race is not merely wrong in theory, will not merely fail in explaining the relations of man to his fellow-man and to the world, but will never even rightly understand the individual upon which it professes to concentrate its whole attention. On the other hand, a mere system of socialism, which ignores the individual or regards him only as an undistinguished part of the whole, will miss some of the most fundamental and characteristic elements which constitute the complete nature of man.

We have already given some attention to the progress of humanity and human civilization as a whole, and we have attempted to show that the highest elements in that civilization are traceable directly to the influence of the Gospel. If we are right in this conclusion, the reason must be found in the fact that Christianity is not merely adapted to teach true principles of sociology, but that its message has also a response to the needs of the individual man. We cannot have a great and noble civilization where individual men are left untaught and uncultivated; neither can the individual attain to his highest and rightful development except amid such circumstances — or, to use the modern phrase, in such an environment — as will favor and foster that development.

We pass therefore, by a natural transition, from the subject of civilization to that of personal culture, — a subject which is receiving at the present moment a very large amount of attention from thinkers, students, and teachers of the most various schools and tendencies. It would perhaps be difficult to mention a subject in which the Church and the world, men of science and men of literature, men who are concerned about education and men who are concerned about government, are more deeply interested.

Man is a living being. Like all living beings, he has a complex nature; and as the highest of them, he has the most complicated nature of all; and this nature is not only capable of cultivation and development, but requires it, and will attain to a complete and harmonious condition just as its culture is legitimate and complete. A plant, a flower, a tree, a bird, a beast, each has its own nature, which will receive its complete harmony and maturity just as it is placed in those circumstances which will provide a supply for all its needs; and so it will be with the crown of animated nature, the being whom we call man. He, too, has powers which must be developed and disciplined in a normal manner, or they will lie dormant or be perverted, so that either partial death or discord and confusion will take the place of life and harmony.[1]

These principles are so universally recognized that the mere statement of them will suffice for our present purpose. As a consequence of the general unanimity on the subject, it has come to pass that each school or system of thought, materialistic or spiritualistic, atheistic or theistic, Christian or unbelieving, has felt bound to work out its own scheme for the education of mankind, for the cultivation of the human powers, with results which are sometimes very remarkably in agreement. Different as their theories of culture are in many respects, they do not very widely disagree with respect to its fruits and its evidences, or even its essential nature. Up to a certain point, indeed, we shall find a very remarkable agreement between the various theories which are proposed for our acceptance.

I. Let us first ask *what those theories are*, and *what they propose to effect*. We have, first, the ordinary worldly or social view of culture, which is purely secular, and which, without condemning or rejecting religion, can hardly be said to take account of it, unless as a mere social fact. We have next the scientific theory, and then the literary theory, respecting which similar remarks may be made. Beyond these we have the con-

---

[1] Aristotle insisted that man, like all other beings, had his own *work* (ἔργον). "Ethics," book i.

fessedly materialistic or atheistic theory. And, apart from these, and in diametrical opposition to some of them, we have the Christian method.

We thoroughly believe that the more carefully we examine the claims and the methods of these theories, the more clearly we shall see that they are reducible to two, — the religious and the unreligious or non-religious, — and that ultimately the various religious theories will be merged in the Christian, in that religion which is based upon the revelation of God in Jesus Christ our Lord. It is quite true that there are systems which will refuse to be assigned to either of these classes, whose advocates imagine that they have made a compromise between mere secularism on the one hand, and a doctrinal Christianity on the other, and so have secured the advantages and avoided the evils of both. But these systems have no inherent vitality. The surrender of distinct Christian doctrine has always led, as all history testifies, to rationalism, to unbelief, to mere deism, and finally to pantheism and atheism.

I. Let us, however, consider some of these theories of human culture just as they present themselves. Let us see what they regard as the essential characteristics of a cultivated human being, and the methods by which they would effect this culture. Now, probably the first thing that will strike us in these theories will be the large extent to which they are in accord with the teachings of the Gospel and the Church. For this agreement we ought, indeed, to be devoutly grateful, being ever ready to recognize the amount of truth which is held by those who differ from ourselves, while we are on our guard against surrendering any portion of that truth which has been delivered to us from above. Let us then proceed to consider the different views of culture which are current among us at the present time.

(1) We take, first, the ordinary worldly, secular, or *social* view of culture. What do men in general mean when they speak of a cultivated person, and what are the qualities by which such an one is generally recognized? The world requires refinement, ease, self-control, gentleness, kindness, courtesy. We can hardly say that the world requires truth, or a high sense of duty, or self-sacrifice. Still it admires these qualities, and applauds them in certain circumstances, especially when they are found in union with those other acquirements and characteristics with which it cannot dispense.

(2) We take next the *scientific* view of culture, and here we will listen to Professor Huxley.[1] "That man, I think, has a liberal education," says Dr. Huxley (his expression is condensed, but not altered), "whose body is the ready servant of his will, . . . whose intellect is a clear,

[1] Lay Sermons, p. 34.

cold logic engine, with all its parts of equal strength and in smooth working order; . . . whose mind is stored with a knowledge of the great and fundamental truths of Nature; . . . one who is full of life and fire, but whose passions are trained to come to heel by a vigorous will, the servant of a tender conscience; who has learned to love all beauty, whether of Nature or of art, to hate all vileness, and to respect others as himself." So much for the scientific view of culture.

(3) What is the *literary* view? There is, perhaps, no one whose right to speak on this point would be considered higher than that of Mr. Matthew Arnold. According to this distinguished writer, culture is " an inward and spiritual activity, having for its characters increased sweetness, increased light, increased life, increased sympathy." Mr. Arnold does not exclude religion as an influence in culture. According to him, religion is "morality touched by emotion."[1] On some parts of these definitions we shall hereafter have to comment. At present we are simply stating the views of the different schools.

(4) It may suffice if we select one other type of teaching on this subject; namely, the positivist, materialistic, or atheistic. There are, of course, positivists and agnostics who are not atheists, who are probably in their hearts theists,

[1] See his "Literature and Dogma" (1873), "God and the Bible" (1875).

although scientifically they will have nothing to do with the region of faith. These, however, are sufficiently represented by the literary and scientific types already noticed. We will now quote the words of one who is a very distinguished as well as a very frank representative of atheism, Dr. Ludwig Büchner, a man of undoubted powers, although sadly lacking in taste. According to this writer,[1] culture (*Bildung*) is "the increased insight of the individual into the ends of civil and social life, increased regard for the rights of others and for his own duties." Elsewhere he includes sympathy among the elements of culture.

2. Now, what is the Christian idea of culture? It is set forth in many different forms in various parts of the Bible. We might specify particularly and supremely the Beatitudes which form the introduction of the Sermon on the Mount as giving the characters of Christian culture in a manner which could hardly be surpassed. The fruits of the Spirit, as enumerated by Saint Paul,[2] run in parallel lines with the precepts of the Divine Master; and the stirring exhortation of Saint Peter[3] in no wise differs from that teaching: "Giving all diligence, add to your faith virtue [manliness]; and to virtue knowledge; and to knowledge temperance; and to temperance patience; and to patience godliness; and to

[1] Der Gottes-Begriff (1874), p. 59.
[2] Gal. v. 22, 23.   [3] 2 Peter i. 5–7.

godliness brotherly kindness; and to brotherly kindness charity."

In all these representations there is a remarkable and striking unity of sentiment such as we should hardly have expected, considering the difference of the points of view from which the subject is regarded. We do not now stop to show that in all of these theories we discern very clearly the influence of the Gospel. At present we will only notice the principal points of agreement between the different theories. Let us note them. All are agreed that in order to a true and liberal human culture, there must be a disciplined and instructed intelligence, a pure and sympathetic heart, and a will strong, benevolent, self-controlled; and that all these powers of man's nature shall be so proportioned and balanced, and so harmonious in their operation, that they shall constitute a character powerful without violence, and gentle without weakness. As to the desirableness of such a character, all respectable men of all schools are wholly agreed. But here a question of the most serious importance meets us.

II. How is such a culture to be attained? It would be wearisome and it is unnecessary even to attempt an enumeration of the various answers which are given to this question. As has been already remarked, there are essentially but two modes of culture. It must be either religious or irreligious; or, if this latter word sounds harsh, let us say non-religious or secular. It must consist in a mere human discipline which has regard only to the laws of Nature, man's bodily and mental constitution and the circumstances in which he is placed; or it must rest upon the revelation of God in our Lord Jesus Christ, the God-man, the Redeemer of the world, and on His redeeming work as applied by the Holy Spirit and by the Christian means of grace.

A believer and teacher of the Gospel of Jesus Christ can, of course, have no difficulty in declaring that, in his judgment at least, a mere secular culture is altogether insufficient and incapable of producing a complete and harmonious development of our powers, such as is the result of the operation of Christian truth in the hearts and minds of those who receive it.

Let it be clearly understood, however, that in pleading for a religious and a Christian discipline, we are in no way attempting to underrate the importance of that training of body and mind which has special regard to the constitution and powers of our human nature, physical and psychical. Those are doing not merely valuable scientific work, but truly divine work, who are engaged in the careful study of the human frame, of the laws of health, and all such subjects. No less are those doing good service to man and to God who are investigating the laws of mind, and treating psychology as an invaluable aid in the work of education. It would be the sheer fanaticism of ignorance which could despise or ignore the importance of such useful and necessary work. Nay, further, we may freely admit that these subjects have been unduly neglected by many advocates of a religious education. By such means they have greatly hindered and marred their own proper work, suffering that nature, which might have been made an auxiliary to grace, to be so burdened and perverted by the neglect of its manifest laws that it has become a great hinderer of the work of the Gospel in the individual life.

While, however, we can regard only with satisfaction every attempt to develop and discipline man's powers of body and mind, we maintain that this cannot be effectually done apart from the influence of religion. For this opinion we will attempt to offer some adequate reasons.

In making this very necessary and serious attempt,—which may God help and prosper and bless!—we must keep clear before us a fundamental principle, already noted, upon which there cannot be, and there is not, any difference of opinion. In order to any true and complete culture, the whole nature of the thing to be cultivated, and not merely a part of it, must be taken into consideration; and provision must be made for the whole of that nature and for all the elements of which it is composed. This is true of every object which is susceptible of cultivation, of the smallest and simplest as well as of the greatest and the most complicated. It is true of the tree, of the plant, of the very grass of the field. It cannot grow, it cannot become what it is capable of becoming, unless it has a suitable soil, a congenial climate, — unless all the circumstances are suited to its nature and requirements. The same principle is applicable to man and to human education. Neglect any part or element of his nature, and the result will be a discipline which is imperfect, one-sided, abnormal.

Now, we venture to assert, having regard to these admitted principles, that a merely secular culture, a culture which knows nothing of God, does not meet the requirements of human nature, and, as a matter of fact, does not produce the rich and beautiful and harmonious results which flow from Christian culture; and that it cannot do so, because it fails to take account of elements in the nature of man which are inseparable from it, and ineradicable.

Such elements are man's longing after God, immortality, perfection, the sense of responsibility, involving the ideas of right and wrong and the consciousness of sin. If these ideas are part of human history and of human nature, can any system which ignores them on principle adequately promote the development and provide for the culture of our human nature? Either it must prove that these ideas are mere illusions, that they are superstitious beliefs engendered by man's fears and ignorance, or else it must confess that it makes no sufficient provision for human culture.

1. Take, first, the notion of immortality. We take it first, because it lies nearest to the truths concerning human nature which all confess, because it does not necessarily involve those higher truths of moral perception, responsibility, dependence upon God, longing for His presence and sustaining power. Undoubtedly it is a notion which can hardly be ignored in considering what is a fitting method of education for a creature like man.

Science tells us that it knows nothing of immortality, and irreligious science declares that the view of life which regards man as destined to exist in a future state of being is quite apart from its calculations and teachings. We know nothing of such prospects, it declares, and we have nothing to do with them. We deal only with acknowledged, tangible facts, which no one can disprove, even if he chooses to ignore them. Yes, we reply; but what if man is an immortal being? What if there is for us human creatures a state of existence after death, into which we must enter after we have done with time? Do you make no provision in your system for such a contingency?

The reply of the non-religious educator is easily anticipated. If, he says, we understand rightly the human constitution, and educate and discipline the individual man in accordance with the laws of his nature, then it does not matter whether his life is limited to this visible sphere or goes on to another existence beyond the grave. If a man is a true man, trained, disciplined, harmoniously developed, then it does not matter where he is or how he is employed. He will be fit, or as fit as he can be, for any position or work to which he may be called.

Undoubtedly there is a large measure of truth in such an answer properly understood. We cannot, however, stop at this point to show the points of our agreement and disagreement with these statements. We will here only ask a question. Does it, then, make no difference to our view of what a man's education ought to be, whether we think his whole life is spent on earth, or he has another life beyond and above the present? Let us put the question still more plainly. If two men take in hand the work of educating a child, and one believes that the death of man on earth is the end of his existence, and the other that it is only the gate of a nobler life, will both of those men conduct the work of education in precisely the same manner? It is impossible that this should be the case. We might as well say that our work in the schoolroom will be precisely the same whether we are to live beyond the age of childhood or not, whether we are ever to grow to manhood or not. For the relation of our future life to the present may be regarded as very similar to the relation of our adult life to the age of childhood. Who does not see that the believer in immortality has many questions to ask which the materialist dismisses with unconcern, and that the answers to these questions will profoundly affect his views of the nature and extent of human education? Certainly a theory of culture which entirely ignores the question of man's immortality can hardly be regarded as sufficient; for most men believe in immortality, and the number of those who do not believe in it or at least regard the question as one worthy of serious consideration must be quite insignificant.

2. But this question is comparatively superficial and preliminary. We have the graver questions of man's relation to the ideas of right and wrong and responsibility and God to consider, before we can determine the true nature of human culture. Now, let the reality of these ideas be once established, and the insufficiency of any merely secular culture becomes at once apparent. In other words, unless these ideas be delusions, and can be proved to be such, no culture short of that which is Christian can be reckoned sufficient, or can actually suffice for human needs.

There are various ways of accounting for the existence of these ideas and for their universal prevalence. The coarse method of denouncing them as the inventions of a priestly caste, which sought power for itself by means of these beliefs among the people, is now very generally abandoned. The mere denunciation of such opinions as gross superstitions, growing up in the midst of a race sunk in ignorance, is partially at least put aside. Yet it is impossible for those who ignore religion as a necessary part of human education to allow ideas of morality and religion to hold their ground without question. Accordingly men of the school of Büchner profess to be able to make short work with all the transcendental, ethical, metaphysical ideas which cannot be accounted for on the mere ground of sensuous experience. There is no such thing as wickedness, they say. Sin as involving guilt or liability to punishment is a mere delusion.[1] Sin is merely ignorance, and ignorance is the fountain of all other evils. Sin is disease, error, desperation. Any idea of a conscience is mere "infant-school morality."[2] And the same must be said of the idea of God. This position has been taken with unusual confidence by some of the most prominent opponents of the existence of God. Thus, Mr. Atkinson and Miss Martineau have declared, in their "Letters," that they do not recognize the existence of morality. Miss Martineau speaks of having "finally dismissed all notion of subjection to a

---

[1] Büchner, Der Gottes-Begriff (1874), p. 60.
[2] Ibid., p. 42.

superior lawless Will, all the perplexing notions of sin and responsibility;" and her master declares that knowledge "sees good in evil and the working of general laws for the general good, and sees no more sin in a crooked disposition than in a crooked stick in the water, or in a humpback or a squint."[1]

Are we ready to accept these statements as a settlement of the question? Apart from our belief, based as we think on abundant evidence, that the Gospel is true, can we, as human beings, who know not only our own instincts, our own needs, our own cravings, but who know that these instincts and cravings belong, broadly speaking, to the whole human race, — can we, with this knowledge, accept undoubtingly the assurance that these ineradicable convictions, not of a few persons here and there, but of the whole human race, have no real foundation to rest upon, — nay, worse, that they are superstitious delusions which stand in the way of a genuine, broad, and liberal culture? Surely not. These convictions of ours are as much matter of fact as any outward object which we have before our eyes. They are as real to us as the craving for food, as the sense of weariness and fatigue, as the joyful consciousness of renewed strength and vigor after repose. And if we are tempted for a moment to doubt our individual conscious-

[1] Letters on the Laws of Man's Nature and Development, by H. G. Atkinson and H. Martineau, p. 141.

ness, it is verified by hundreds, by thousands, by millions of our fellow-men.

(1) Take the case of *conscience*. A sense of right and wrong is the universal possession of humanity. In some persons and in some races it is very feeble. In some persons it is totally lacking. But this no more proves that man has not a conscience, than the existence of idiots or madmen proves that man has no intelligence, is not a rational being. How do those who deny that conscience is an element in the actual constitution of man account for its existence? It is, they say, the result of education, not merely of the individual, but of the race. The so-called moral ideas have been generated in the long course of human history. In the struggle for existence, in the endeavor to preserve what they had acquired, men had to inflict suffering upon those who sought to injure them. Out of the need of protection arose governments which had to punish those who infringed their rules; and in this way there arose a sense of evil doing, the hurting of others was known to be a thing which entailed some kind of retribution upon the author of the injury, and thus the ideas of right and wrong and innocence and guilt were generated in the race.[1]

It is impossible to deny the measure of truth which is contained in this explanation of man's moral being. Without education we should

[1] Compare H. Spencer's "Data of Ethics."

probably not be moral beings at all. But the same is true of our rational nature. If it were possible to separate a child at its birth from all human and educational influences, that child would grow up hardly different from a brute. If such a case were found, should we have a right to say that this particular human being was not rational? Should we have a right to put it in the class of the brute creation? Certainly not. We should know that the nature was there, although undeveloped,—that, if it had been properly educated, it would have come forth into activity, as in the case of men who received a normal training. We know, too, that no amount of training or education or discipline would develop intelligence in the mere brute. Here, therefore, there is an original, essential difference between the man and the mere animal. The one may, by neglect, be allowed to fall back almost to the level of the other. By no possibility can the brute be developed into the man.

It is the same with the moral nature. Unless it had in man a real existence, it could not be educated. You cannot produce the sense of right and wrong in the mere brute, although in various ways that sense may be destroyed in man. Let us grant that, as a matter of fact, the state of our conscience, like the condition of our reason, is the result of education. Our moral life begins with the utterances of authority. We believe what we are told as to right and wrong. But we do not believe unquestioningly. We bring the judgments and teachings of others before the bar of our own judgment and conscience, and test them by our own reason and moral sense. And when we have once acquired the convictions which are partly the result of education, partly the outcome of our own thought, we no more can part with them, unless some injury is inflicted upon our moral nature, than we can part with the principles of accurate thinking, unless our intellect is destroyed.

Men do not know the rules of the syllogism by intuition. As a matter of fact, many men violate them without any consciousness of thinking inaccurately. Let them, however, get clearly to understand those rules, and they can no more deny them than they can deny their own existence. So with the moral perceptions by which men are lighted in the life of duty. In one sense they are intuitive; they are not the result of any process of reasoning, they shine by their own light. Yet there are men who have possessed them in very slight measure, and we may admit the possibility of men being found in whom they have no place. When, however, the conscience has once been educated to discern between good and evil, it retains its moral vision; it will not be driven from its new post of vantage unless some great injury is inflicted upon the constitution to which it belongs.

Can we, then, believe that conscience is a mere accident in human nature, generated by circumstances and by experience; or are we driven to the conclusion that it is an elementary ✓ part of the constitution of man? We cannot hesitate as to which of these opinions we should adopt. Our reason unites with our inward consciousness in the testimony that we are moral beings, lighted by the lamp of righteousness and duty, constrained by an inner law to walk in that light which shines upon us from a higher world.

(2) It may be safely said that, ultimately, the idea of conscience and the *idea of God* will stand ✓ or fall together in the same mind and in the same society. If there is nothing in the universe but matter, if thought is a mere attribute of matter and the result of its organization, then the idea of God is forever banished from the realm of thought, and conscience can be no ✓ more than the description of a state which is the result of a certain kind of culture.

This subject will be considered, in its speculative aspect, more particularly, in the lecture on Materialism. At present we have to deal with it more immediately as a practical question. That the idea of God is almost universal among men, no one thinks of denying. That it is almost inseparable from the idea of right and wrong, is equally certain. Indeed, the great German metaphysician, Kant, found in the certainty and authority of conscience the one conclusive proof of the existence of God. The "categorical imperative" of the conscience was the supreme, undeniable truth in the constitution of man, and drew after it, as a necessity, a belief in the existence of a supreme Lawgiver and Judge. Doubtless it is this inner witness to truth and goodness, this inner judge which refuses to resolve all human action into a mere calculation of consequences, into a mere question of profit and loss, and demands that men shall do right and shall not do wrong, which makes men hesitate to believe that there is no God. At any rate, few men will avow such a belief, and even those who will not maintain the affirmative on this question will generally take refuge in the plea of ignorance.

Men like Dr. Büchner are bolder. The idea of God, in their view, is as much a childish superstition as the idea of sin. It is the offspring of ignorance and fear.[1] Petronius, according to him, was right when he said that Fear was the first maker of Gods in the world ("Primus in orbe Deos fecit timor"). Mr. Mill,[2] who seems to have had Büchner as well as Petronius in his mind, remarks: "The old saying, 'Primus in orbe Deos fecit timor,' I hold to be untrue, or to contain, at most, only a small amount

[1] Büchner, "Der Gottes-Begriff" (1874), p. 14. Compare his "Kraft und Stoff:" "Die Gottes-Idee."
[2] Three Essays on Religion, by J. S. Mill, p. 100.

of truth. Belief in gods had, I conceive, even in the rudest minds, a more honorable origin."

It certainly does seem strange that Dr. Büchner should assign such a parentage to an idea which, he tells us, here agreeing with all trustworthy witnesses, is wanting among certain barbarous nations, but is the common possession of all civilized peoples. The idea of God and of duty does not die out of men's minds as they advance in knowledge and in civilization. It grows deeper and stronger and more tenacious. Man feels — and no amount of civilization can educate him out of the feeling — that he needs God. "If God did not exist," said Voltaire, "it would be necessary to invent him." He little thought how soon his saying would be verified. The French people at the Revolution professed to abolish the Deity along with the historical institutions of their country. But they found they could live longer without the government of kings than they could without the worship of Almighty God. The restoration of religion, in some shape, was effected long before the restoration of monarchy. Robespierre sent the revolutionary atheists to the guillotine, and celebrated the festival of the Supreme Being.[1] It is a striking comment on the boast that the hypothesis of a Deity is as unnecessary in human life as it is in physical science.

[1] June 8, 1794. Thiers, "French Revolution," chap. xxxv.

(3) We have just referred to the assertion that the idea of God was the child of ignorance and fear. This is glaringly untrue; but it has a measure of truth lying near to it. Man's fears of God would rather lead him to cast doubts upon the fact of the Divine existence. But conscience is too strong for his sophistry and casuistry. His fears do constrain him to ask whether God has revealed Himself, how He is disposed towards man, and in what way His offending creatures may draw near to Him.

For men are conscious of sin, are troubled by the thought of guilt, of a past which they cannot efface, by the consciousness of a present feebleness which they cannot cure, by the prospect of a future which is all unknown. Look at these facts of human consciousness, and consider their bearing on this subject of culture. What possibility is there of a free and broad culture in a soil so choked with weeds? This sense of guilt, this inner grief which darkens all the higher life, is an effectual barrier against the entrance of the influences which would foster and strengthen and discipline the powers of the soul. There can be no true freedom, and therefore no harmonious development, expansion, until the soul knows of a God who is a Father, pardoning, helping, blessing.

It is for this reason that we believe no true halting-place can be found between materialism and the Gospel, between the system which ignores God and the system which tells us authoritatively how we may be at peace with God. Deism has been tried over and over again. It has been weighed in the balances and found wanting. Deism cannot even deliver us from any of the difficulties supposed to be connected with the Christian Revelation. The late Mr. Mill has told us in his Autobiography,[1] that, as against the deist, Bishop Butler's argument is irresistible. Grant the existence of a God, and take the world as it is, and there is no difficulty in the Christian Revelation which does not meet us when we regard the world in which we live as the sphere of Divine government. We shall not escape the difficulties of belief by surrendering the Christian Revelation and falling back upon the belief in a God who is revealed only in nature, in history, and in conscience.

(4) But although we shall gain nothing by adopting deism instead of Christianity, we shall lose much by the exchange. There is no other religion which even professes to do what the Gospel promises to those who become followers of the Christ. Suppose we undertake the education of a human being, and begin by asking where and how he may obtain a clear light to guide him through the intricacies of " this troublesome world," how he may free his inner man from the cloud of guilt which broods over it, how he may obtain strength to fight the

[1] He repeats it in his " Essays on Religion," p. 214.

battle of life, — in short, how he may so free all the powers of his nature from impediments which check their exercise, how he may introduce into them a principle which shall reduce them to harmony and at the same time stimulate them to work, — what system is there on earth that professes to give answers to questions like these? Is it enough to listen to the positivist, and hear that we know only matter and its qualities, while we are forced to believe in some mysterious force pervading all matter, of which, however, we can have no certain knowledge? Will such an assurance strike the shackles off the wrists of men who are in spiritual bondage, or restore the spiritual paralytic to sound health and vigor? Shall we obtain a more satisfactory answer from the modern apostle of culture without Christianity, who tells us that God is "a power or stream of tendency not ourselves which makes for righteousness," and that religion is "morality touched with emotion"? Imagine Saint Paul giving this answer to the agonized conscience asking what must be done in order that it might be saved! Imagine this for an answer: "Believe in a power not yourself which makes for righteousness, and practise a morality which is not a mere hard, dry conformity to law, but a morality which is lightened by sentiment and emotion!" This is certainly a strange way of setting men free, and sending them on their way rejoicing.

(5) We know what the Gospel professes to do for men, and we know also what it has done. We know what it did for Saint Paul nearly two thousand years ago; we know what it did for Luther nearly four hundred years ago, and what it has done for many more before and after the days of the great Reformer. Certainly our Lord has not left Himself without witnesses of the truth of His promises,— of the reality of the blessings which He professed to prepare for those who received His message. We have a double testimony to His fidelity. We have the history of the Christian society in its onward progress from the day of Pentecost to this hour, and we have the testimony of the manifested lives and of the inward experience of individual Christians. We believe that there is no comparison between the Christian life, whether seen in the individual or in society, and the life of those who are "without Christ."

We do not, of course, deny that there have been many eminent and highly cultivated men who have lived "without God in the world," and have passed away without faith or hope in His promises, or even in His existence. It may be that instances can be found, in the history of mankind, of high moral as well as intellectual qualities in those who have had no religious beliefs or principles. But we may safely assert that such are to be found chiefly among those who have indirectly come under religious, and especially under Christian, influences; further, that such cases are exceptional; and finally, that even the best of such examples are found defective when compared with the noblest examples of Christian culture.

We have already referred to the Autobiography of Mr. John Mill, one of the most eminent representatives of the secular school, and a distinguished writer. Let any thoughtful person read that book, and we are quite sure what his judgment will be when he is asked whether he could believe that a Christian would gain anything, socially and morally, by abandoning his faith in Christ and adopting the principles of that eminent man's life.

It will, however, be better to draw our illustration from another people. One of the most splendid examples of a merely worldly culture was undoubtedly the great German, J. W. Goethe. He was a man who in certain respects was inferior to none in the fascination which he exercised over some of the most distinguished men of his age. It is not difficult to account for this influence. He was one of the wonders of his time. His physical beauty, his capacious intellect, his harmonious culture, his serene self-satisfaction and calm self-idolatry, formed a combination which with most men proved overpowering. Yet study his character in the admirable English biography of him,[1] and

[1] Lewes's Life of Goethe.

ask whether you would really desire to be such an one as he. The cold selfishness which was his strongest moving principle strikes upon the heart which has been touched by the love of Christ like a wind that comes from fields of ice and snow. The whole life of the man revolved round self. How could it be otherwise when he was ignorant of the true centre of universal being? One of the most eminent of his contemporaries, Friedrich Schiller, wrote thus of him : " To be frequently with Goethe would make me wretched. Even with his nearest friends he has no self-forgetfulness, no effusion; he is in no ordinary degree an egotist."[1]

Even the author of " Natural Religion," while extolling some of the "great and rare virtues" of Goethe, is constrained to admit that "there remains the fact that the idea of duty and self-sacrifice appears not to be very sacred to his mind, — rather, perhaps, to be irritating, embarrassing, odious to him."[2]

Compare this character for a moment with that of a man belonging to a nation which, as a whole, in a moral view compares unfavorably with the German, — Saint François de Sales, the saintly Bishop of Geneva. Saint Francis was also a man of the highest culture and of the

[1] Quoted in Hamberger's "Christenthum und moderne Cultur," bd. i. s. 12. The view of Goethe's character given in Mr. Hutton's delightful essay (vol. ii. Essay 1) does not differ from this, and deserves careful study.

[2] Natural Religion, part i. chap. v. p. 98.

most remarkable powers of fascination, although he had derived his power from a very different source. Let these two men be compared, and then let us say whether secularism or Christianity produces the finer and richer fruits. It would be easy to mention bishops of our own race no less remarkable than the Bishop of Geneva. Let any one, however, compare the Christian Savoyard with the mere man of culture, perhaps the most perfect specimen of the kind which Germany or the world has produced, and let him mark that the humility, the sweetness, the tenderness, the burning love of the Christian, have all been acquired in the school of " Jesus Christ and Him crucified."

Shall we, for a moment, go to France for the man of worldly culture and to Germany for the Christian? There are few more eminent in his own way than Jean Jacques Rousseau. And this is what one of his countrymen says of him: " Life without actions; life entirely resolved into affections and half-sensual thoughts; do-nothingness setting up for a virtue; cowardliness with voluptuousness; fierce pride with nullity underneath it . . . there is Rousseau!" Such is the judgment pronounced on Rousseau by Michelet in his " Life of Luther." This is the man who said of his own " Confessions:" "Let the trumpet of judgment sound when it may, I will come with this book in my hand and challenge any one present to say, if he dare, ' I was better than that man.'" No wonder that Michelet, when endeavoring to set forth the greatness of the character of the Christian Luther, should think of this wretched unbeliever as a contrast. Certainly we should hardly think of the robust Thuringian peasant and monk as an example of the highest culture; and yet who does not feel that the words spoken by him, in prospect of that dread day of trial, are the utterance of a finer spirit? "When I think of it," he says, "I feel that I could pass a sponge over all that I have written. To have to render to God an account of every idle word, — it is terrible!"

But the influence of Christianity is seen not merely in the choicest examples of its power, but in every society into which it has entered. The Gospel has created a new morality among men, and the Church has been the source of streams of mercy and blessing which have flowed forth upon the poor and miserable with healing, restoring, and regenerating power. Christianity has given to the world a type of character unknown to heathenism, a type of such lofty and ideal beauty as man had never before even conceived. If the Christian ideal of life were abolished, suppressed, forgotten, — if the life and character of Christ were blotted out from human consciousness, — what is there in the world which could be counted worthy to take its place? Whence but from Jesus could we learn the lesson of profound humility, of loving gentleness and patience, of glorious self-sacrifice, which constitute the most lovely elements in the noblest of human characters?

"It was reserved for Christianity," says Mr. Lecky,[1] and he is no over-partial witness, "to present to the world an ideal character, which through all the changes of eighteen centuries has inspired the hearts of men with an impassioned love; has shown itself capable of acting on all ages, nations, temperaments, and conditions; has been not only the highest pattern of virtue, but the strongest incentive to its practice; and has exercised so deep an influence that it may be truly said that the simple record of three short years of active life has done more to regenerate and to soften mankind than all the disquisitions of philosophers, and all the exhortations of moralists."

We have already spoken of the belief in a future life as affecting our view of the nature of that culture which is adapted for creatures like ourselves. But there is another consideration connected with the expectation of immortality; we refer to its power as a motive of action. Even Mr. Mill allows that the "supernatural religions must always possess" one advantage "over the religion of humanity,—the prospect that they hold out to the individual

[1] History of European Morals, vol. ii. chap. iv. p. 8, Amer. ed.; p. 9, Eng. 8vo ed.

of a life after death;" and he afterwards admits, that, "if there is nothing to prove" the reality of this hope, "there is as little in our knowledge and experience to contradict it."[1] But surely it must be apparent that a merely secular culture provides only for the present life, and, in carrying on its work, can derive no help from a motive which has seldom altogether lost its power among men.

But again we must remind ourselves that there is only One who professes to give us certain knowledge concerning the life to come. It is "our Saviour Jesus Christ, who hath abolished death, and hath brought life and immortality to light through the Gospel."[2] He has gone through the gates of death into the land of everlasting life, and He has said what He alone had the right to say, "Where I am, there shall also My servant be." "I go to prepare a place for you."[3] It is not that we would base the claims of Christ either on our hopes or on our fears for the future alone. Jesus Christ has claims upon us apart from His promise of a future life of blessedness. Even if He were not the Saviour of sinners, He would still be the highest and the noblest of men. Even if He were not the King of Angels, seated on the throne of heaven, He would at least be the Sovereign of Humanity, whose image is

[1] Three Essays, pp. 118, 120.
[2] 2 Tim. i. 10.   [3] John xii. 26; xiv. 2.

enshrined within the heart of every noblest, truest, purest man and woman. And he who seeks to follow the highest ideal of human culture, he who endeavors to realize that ideal in his own life, will at least desire and strive to know Him more perfectly.

On this subject one writer of eminence has been quoted. Let us listen to another much further removed from the faith of the Church; let us listen once more to Mr. J. S. Mill. "About the life and sayings of Jesus," he remarks, "there is a stamp of personal originality, combined with profundity of insight, which . . . must place the Prophet of Nazareth . . . in the very first rank of the men of sublime genius of whom our species can boast. When this preeminent genius is combined with the qualities of probably the greatest moral reformer and martyr to that mission, who ever existed upon earth, religion cannot be said to have made a bad choice in pitching on this man as the ideal representative and guide of humanity; nor, even now, would it be easy, even for an unbeliever, to find a better translation of the rule of virtue from the abstract into the concrete, than to endeavor so to live that Christ would approve our life." [1]

If among those who are listening to these words there are, unhappily, any present who own no allegiance to Him who has seldom failed

---

[1] Three Essays, pp. 254, 255.

to extort homage, even from His adversaries, let them, for their own souls' sake, pause and ask themselves whether, in the cultivation of their minds and in the conduct of their lives, it is wise to ignore such an influence as His. But, beyond all this, they may well inquire, further, whether He may not have claims upon them which are not only strong and binding in time, but which remain unexhausted throughout eternity.

LECTURE IV.

THE UNITY OF CHRISTIAN DOCTRINE.

Does the Bible teach definite Religious Truth? — Denied. — What may be meant by the Denial? — Divine Revelation in Christ. — Gradually unfolded. — True Development. — Illustrated in the Writings of Saint Paul. — Later Examples of Development in the History of the Church. — Schools of Thought. — Development and Accretion distinguished. — Illustrations of Unity in Christian Teaching: 1. The Nature of God. — Represented as possessing Human Attributes and as being far removed from Humanity. — Deistic and Pantheistic Conceptions. — 2. The Character of God. — Divine Decrees and Human Liberty. — 3. The Nature of Man. — Original Sin. — Concupiscence. — 4. Eschatology. Future Retribution. — Three current Theories. — Not absolutely Irreconcilable. — Analogy of the Book of Nature and Science with the Book of Grace and Theology.

WHAT is Truth? Is there such a thing apart from the individual mind? Can we speak of objective truth, or is it only subjective, — that which every individual mind troweth? And if there is such a thing as definite scientific truth, is there also spiritual truth? Is there such a thing as definite religious doctrine, which must be accepted as the true representation of supernatural facts and relations, without alteration or modification?

Further, if there is such a thing as objective religious truth, does the Bible[1] contain it and declare it? Has the Gospel message anything definite, unchangeable, permanent; or does it merely consist of a set of propositions, more or less indefinite and vague, which each age modifies for itself according to its own point of view and its own moral education?

These are important questions; and they are of special importance at the present time, when it is stoutly maintained that the Bible does not set forth or compel assent to any particular truths or dogmas, but that it yields up to each age, to each society, and almost to each individual, very nearly what they please,—in short, that men bring their opinions to the Bible, instead of seeking guidance from it; that they simply search the Scriptures, not that they may learn and humbly accept the truth which they contain, but that they may find texts and passages which they will be able to quote in confirmation of conclusions at which they have already arrived.

It is easy to exaggerate these accusations, and they have been brought forward in very exaggerated forms. But we must grant that they rest upon a foundation of truth. And it

---

[1] It will be observed that, in the present series of lectures, no notice is taken of the scientific objections to the historical character of the early books of the Old Testament. On this point see Note D.

will be our business to show that the amount of truth which they contain is not at variance with our assertion of the *Unity of Christian Doctrine.* It may, therefore, be as well that we should at once declare what we mean by conceding that there has been a great variety of Christian teaching, sometimes even apparently contradictory teaching, and this not merely from those whom the Church has branded as heretics, but proceeding from teachers regarded as Orthodox; and further that we should explain in what sense we assert the unity of Christian teaching and the authority of the Bible as the source from which that teaching has been derived.

That Christian truth has presented itself in the same form in all ages of the world, no reasonable and instructed Christian will think of maintaining. Different aspects of truth have been prominent in different periods of the Church's history; and there has been a certain development or unfolding of doctrinal truth, in the past ages of the Church, which may perhaps be going on at this moment, and which may be continued in the future history of religious thought. In this supposition there is nothing unreasonable, there is nothing disrespectful to the original sacred deposit, and there is nothing in the least degree inconsistent with the unity of Christian doctrine.

It is of the nature of all deeper truths to be many-sided, to reveal themselves by slow degrees, to be clearer to some minds than to others, to be lost and recovered by different men and different ages. And this, which is true of truth in general, may well be predicated of that truth and those doctrines which are the vehicles of a Divine Revelation, — which convey to us the thoughts of God concerning His own nature, character, will; which tell us of our relations to Him, and which lay down the duties which flow from those relations. And all this is quite consistent with a belief in the unity of Christian doctrine.

I. Let us remember that, according to the Christian belief, God has revealed Himself to man in the person of the Incarnate Word, in a human life; that He has caused the story of that life, its words, its deeds, and its sufferings, to be recorded for our instruction; further, that He has imparted to authorized ambassadors a supernatural power, by which they have been enabled to explain to us the meaning of that life and work, and of the organization, the Christian Church, in which its blessings were to be enjoyed, and by which its privileges were to be conveyed to mankind; and then we shall be better prepared to understand the process by which these truths have been diffused in the world and received among men.

In the first place, it is a revelation of God which is the subject of these testimonies, — a revelation of the Eternal and Infinite, made in such a form as to be intelligible to us, the temporal and finite, and to all kinds of men among us, the simple and the most childlike as well as the wisest and the most subtle. Let us remember this, and we shall have no difficulty in understanding in what various degrees these heavenly truths will stand out and be grasped and perceived by different classes of minds and in different ages of the world.

The statement might be illustrated in a thousand ways, from many different departments of human life. Although we have not here to do specially, or in any direct sense at all, with the Old Testament, we might for a moment draw an illustration from the writings which it contains. The Law, the Prophets, the Psalms, show a remarkable development of spiritual truth, communicated to those who lived under the earlier economy, from the time when sacrifices were ordained as teachers of moral and spiritual truth, and simple general duties were laid down in bare precepts, to the time when it was shown that no sacrifices were of any real value in the sight of God but those which were spiritual in their nature, and that those simple precepts of early ages must be referred to eternal principles from which they drew their authority and their sanction.

Or again, if we turn to the New Testament, we shall find the same order of proceeding. It is believed by those who have most deeply studied the writings of the New Covenant that the germs of all spiritual truth are to be found in the teaching of our Lord. And yet it would have been very difficult for us to obtain from His words many of the truths which we have learned from the teaching of the Apostles. And He Himself indicated that such was the case, and gave the reason for the method which He pursued.

He told His disciples in His valedictory address:[1] "I have yet many things to say unto you, but ye cannot bear them now. Howbeit, when He, the Spirit of truth, is come, He shall guide you into all the truth. . . . He shall glorify Me: for He shall take of Mine, and shall declare it unto you." And we see how this promise was fulfilled in the later Books of the New Testament. In the Acts of the Apostles, for instance, the Apostles received guidance, as they needed it, concerning the reception of the Gentiles into the Church and the rules to be imposed upon them. But it is especially in the Apostolic epistles that we see the glorious fulfilment of this promise.

In the earlier revelation God had taught men "by divers portions and in divers manners,"[2] but in the later He spoke to them "by His Son." There was a unity as well as a fulness in the later revelation, distinguishing it as a full

---

[1] John xvi. 12, ff. (Revised Version).
[2] Heb. i. 1, 2.

splendor of truth from the scattered rays which had come before. But still there were needed many different media of communication, and a gradual and progressive teaching, before the complete truth could shine into our minds. Even those who maintain that Saint James, Saint Paul, Saint Peter, and Saint John show different religious tendencies, are still witnesses to the fact that different aspects of truth were presented to the Church from the beginning; and we who believe that there is a most perfect harmony between these early inspired teachers may be encouraged to seek for a fundamental unity of doctrine in the later teachings of Christendom.

There is, indeed, something very beautiful in what we may call the progress of doctrine in the writings of Saint Paul. In his earlier epistles, those to the Galatians and Romans, he deals with the question of personal acceptance with God, the first question that must be dealt with in announcing a message of good news from God; in the later, those to the Ephesians and Colossians, he teaches a more advanced doctrine concerning the Church as the Body of Christ, in which all believers are members; while the Epistle to the Philippians forms a kind of transition from the one to the other. And yet there is absolutely no discord; there is a perfect harmony between this later teaching and the earlier. For in the Epistle to the Ephesians the doctrine of the early epistles is clearly asserted: "By grace are ye saved through faith;"[1] and the distinctive teaching of the later epistle concerning the Body[2] of Christ is foreshadowed in the Epistle to the Romans, where Christians are declared to be "one body in Christ, and severally members one of another,"[3] and even in the teaching of our Lord, as recorded by Saint John, where He says: "I am the vine, ye are the branches."[4] So in the epistles of Saint John, there is a wonderful depth and fulness of teaching concerning our abiding in Christ, and the life of which we are partakers by reason of that indwelling, and of the Love which is the life of God and of man.

If we might, for a moment, bring forward a parallel example of this progress of doctrine in the Church, we should find it by comparing the prevailing teaching at the time of the Reformation, or at the beginning of the evangelical revival in the eighteenth century, with that type of doctrine which is most prominent in the writings of the more thoughtful divines in Great Britain and in America at the present time. When the Reformation was under the guidance of its greatest representative, Martin Luther, nearly all the distinctive truths upon which he insisted were supported mainly by quotations from the Epistles to the Galatians and to the

[1] Eph. ii. 8.
[2] Eph. i. 23; ii. 6; iv. 4, 16; v. 30.
[3] Rom. xii. 5. [4] John xv. 1–8.

Romans. It was quite natural that it should be so. The urgent question of that time was: How shall a man be just with God? How was personal justification to be secured? And it was very much the same in the evangelical revival of the last century. Religion had been merged in morality, and men were awakened to ask whether this was all, whether there was any question as to their being right with God. The answers to these questionings were to be found in the clear enunciation of the conditions on which those who had sinned could be accepted with God; and for this men turned naturally, almost necessarily, to the early epistles of Saint Paul.

But a change has come over the type of our ordinary teaching in these later days, and other aspects of Divine truth are brought into greater prominence. We are now seeing that religion is not a mere personal, individual matter, but that it is also corporate and social; moreover, we get beyond the point of view of justification, and are led into the deeper truths so powerfully brought out by Saint John, — the truths of life in God and of communion with Him and with His Son Jesus Christ. And yet there is no want of harmony in these different aspects of truth. The circle of Divine Revelation would be incomplete if any portion of this teaching were withdrawn from it; and we are coming, more and more, to perceive that all these phases of doctrine are but rays from the central sun of truth, which must be brought into a focus before we can know all that God would reveal to us of His own character and work.

There is, however, another way in which these different phases of teaching present themselves to us in the history of the Church. They appear in Christian teaching, not merely as successive developments of truth, or as those aspects of truth which satisfy different ages, but as distinguishing different schools of thought, which are sometimes distinctive of different nationalities, and are the result of different providential and educational training, and sometimes appear side by side in the same country and in the same age, having, as it would appear, a special correspondence with the peculiar intellectual type or the special religious experience of those by whom they are received or taught.

One of the most remarkable illustrations of these diverse types of Christian truth, neither of which presents any real deflection from the general Christian tradition or the accepted doctrine of the Church, is to be found in the Alexandrian School of Clement and Origen on the one hand, and the Augustinian School on the other. The characteristics of these schools are strongly and clearly marked. The one has its origin in the sombre African theology of Tertullian and Cyprian, and in the logical and rhetorical discipline of the great Augustine. The other derives its characteristic tendencies from Philo and the followers of Plato in general. It is beyond our present purpose to point out, in detail, the distinctive differences of these schools, which have recently been made the subject of careful investigation.[1] Generally speaking, the Alexandrian School represents that side of Christian teaching which takes a favorable view of human philosophy and even of non-Christian religions, regarding the truth which they contain as part of the light derived by mankind from the eternal Word; while the Augustinians would draw more attention to the errors of human systems, as being the work of sin and the devil. So, too, the Alexandrian School would seem to know little of those darker views of human nature apart from the grace of Christ, which were promulgated by Augustine, and which, from him, became part of the accredited teaching of the Western Church. To some of these points we shall hereafter draw attention. At present it may be sufficient to remark, that, while the Alexandrians mainly preserved the traditional teaching of Saint John, the Augustinians were profoundly Pauline in their conceptions. In nearly every age these two tendencies may be traced in the Christian Church; although, as we

[1] The reader may be referred to the "Continuity of Christian Thought," by the Rev. A. V. G. Allen; and to the "Christian Platonists of Alexandria" (Bampton Lectures for 1886), by Dr. Charles Bigg.

have remarked, one may be more prominent at one time and another at another. In our own day the Johannean tendency is conspicuous in the disciples of Schleiermacher, Coleridge, and Maurice; while the Augustinian School has two conspicuous representatives in the Puritan Calvinistic School and in the Churchly School,—the one embodied in the evangelical revival and its legitimate descendants; the other in the Oxford movement and in the whole rising of the idea of corporate life, which is so potent an ingredient in contemporary religious thought. As we have said, these different tendencies come before us sometimes as a process of development, sometimes as representative of different schools of thought. But in either case they rest upon the same basis of fundamental truth; and amid all their superficial differences there is a marvellous unity distinguishable in the inner kernel which they contain.

But here it may be necessary to point out somewhat more exactly what we mean by the development of doctrine, since it may appear to some that we are, by using such an expression, disguising a fictitious unity by making it appear real. And this has become the more necessary, since new forms of Christian doctrines have, in recent times, been brought forward as developments of the original deposit, when they have in fact been accretions,—doctrines and opinions superinduced upon the old, and not drawn from it by any legitimate process of deduction or development. An illustration of the two methods may be found in the Nicene doctrine of the Person of Christ on the one hand, and in the Vatican doctrine of papal infallibility on the other. The one is lawful development, the explicit enunciation of a doctrine which had been implictly taught from the beginning. The other is unlawful accretion, being a doctrine utterly unknown in the first ages of the Church and for many an age afterwards, having no faintest germ of its life in the writings of the Apostles or of the first Fathers and teachers and witnesses of the Church and its doctrines. The Nicene Fathers simply added new definitions, rendered necessary by the attacks made upon the doctrine of the Church. They did not mean to add, and they did not in fact add, one jot or one tittle to the faith which they had received; they simply surrounded it with such safeguards that no one could deny it without assailing the definite decisions of the Church. It was widely different with the Vatican decree. It was not even a necessary development of the Roman theory of papal supremacy; while that doctrine in its turn was a pure invention, having no germinal truth corresponding with it which was known in the Church in the Nicene period or even a century later. In all the legitimate developments of Christian doctrine, so far as they have been embodied in the authorized documents of the Church, there is a conspicuous unity; and the same may be said of much of the teaching which has been commended by the greater minds of the Christian Church, but which has never received the final impress of ecclesiastical authority.

II. It is, of course, impossible to draw out in detail proofs or illustrations of these statements. But there is no difficulty in giving specimens of the unity in the midst of variety and diversity by which Christian teaching has been distinguished; and these samples shall be selected from those teachings which have been adduced by objectors who complained of the want of definiteness and harmony in the utterances of Christian teachers. Let us note some of these allegations as they regard the nature and character of God, the nature and future destiny of man.

1. With regard to the *nature of God*. It has been alleged, and with no small appearance of truth, that representations of the Almighty have been given by Christian teachers and even by Holy Scripture itself which cannot be reconciled, which are indeed mutually contradictory. For example, it has been represented, on the one hand, that the Most High is invested with attributes similar to those possessed by men, or even identical with them, even to the very emotions and passions which belong to the weakest and most variable side of our human

nature; while, on the other hand, He has been represented as One who is lifted high above all human emotions and passions, being pure Spirit, and sometimes as mere Negation. Again, there has been a teaching, either purely pantheistic or partaking of a pantheistic tendency, which has spoken of the Almighty God as immanent in the universe, as pervading all existence and forming its ground and support; and this teaching has drawn its proofs from Holy Scripture. On the other hand, another class of teachers, with a deistic tendency, have represented the Almighty as transcending the universe, being distinct, if not separate, from the works of His hands; and these too have quoted Scripture in support of their assertions. To the one class belong Christian teachers of the school of Schleiermacher and Coleridge; to the other belong the deists of the last century, the influence of whom is perceptible even in orthodox writers like Butler and Paley.

It might seem presumptuous, and even in a measure supercilious, for any one to assume a position of mediation between schools so widely separated as those which have been mentioned; and if the mediation were merely that of an individual, he could scarcely defend himself from the charge of arrogance. When, however, we assert our belief that Almighty God has, by means of these diverse and conflicting efforts, been leading His Church to higher and wider and deeper views of His own nature, we may hope not only to escape from such a charge, but to gain credence from those who consider that it is in this way that larger and fuller truth has been gained on every subject of human inquiry. We cannot doubt that it is so, and that it will increasingly be found to be so, in regard to our knowledge of the Divine nature and relations to the universe.

" Who by searching can find out God?" We feel sure *that* God is: we cannot perfectly tell *what* He is. When we say He is absolute, infinite, eternal, we are simply removing Him from the sphere of human definition. To define is to limit. In so far, we must all confess ourselves to be, in a sense, Christian agnostics. Yet we do feel that those anthropomorphic expressions concerning the Most High, which are found in Holy Scripture and in our popular theology, do contain such measure of truth as we are able, in certain stages of our spiritual development, to receive concerning the nature and will of God. And further, that these phrases are not merely statements upon which we can base our practical action, but that they do actually represent truth concerning the nature of God, because we believe that we are made in the Divine image. There is nothing in our nature, apart from its sinfulness, which has not its archetype in God; and although no language which we could understand may be capable of telling us what

God is in Himself, yet such expressions may bring to our minds such true knowledge as we are capable of receiving.

Take, again, the apparently conflicting representations of the deistic and pantheistic teachers. If these statements are considered as negations, the one denying the immanence and the other the transcendence, then, of course, they are contradictory and irreconcilable. If, however, the theologian of deistic tendencies merely asserts that God is not contained in the universe, but transcends it, then he is declaring a truth which is established alike by Scripture and reason; and if the theologian of pantheistic tendencies maintains that God is in all things and through all things, that in Him we live and move and have our being, then he, too, is declaring a plain truth of Scripture which is acknowledged by the most profound and the most spiritual philosophy. So far are these two truths from being contradictory that we seem now to be agreed that their synthesis brings us as near as we can come to a true view of the relation of the Almighty to the universe which He originated and which He governs.

2. When we come to consider what may be more precisely described as the *character* of God, we are confronted by a strange opposition between different representations of His loving purposes towards mankind. On the one side we have the various Augustinian and Calvinistic

schools, with their doctrines of Election and Reprobation or Preterition; and on the other, the school of Alexandria, the Pelagian, semi-Pelagian, and Arminian schools, which either know nothing of such predestination or are vehemently opposed to the Augustinian doctrine. Here surely is discord beyond all hope of conciliation or harmony. Statements confronting each other as contraries or contradictories cannot logically be brought into agreement; and here it might seem hopeless to establish any unity of teaching.

It must, indeed, be conceded that, if we are to take the mere utterances, formal conclusions, and arguments of these schools, we shall fail to discover any harmony or unity in their teaching. But this will not be the case if we penetrate beneath the surface, and lay hold of the fundamental principles for which these opposite schools were contending. On the one hand, the sovereignty of God is a self-evident fact. On the other hand, there can be no human responsibility apart from rational, moral liberty. In whatever degree you limit a man's liberty, in that degree you limit his responsibility. These two sets of truths are, in reality, self-evident. If we cannot reconcile them we must leave them where they are, for we cannot blot them out.

Again, the Arminian and others of his way of thinking may contend — and the human conscience will go with them in the contention — that no man can be responsible for doing what God has decided and decreed that he shall not do, and what it was impossible for him to do unless God had decreed otherwise ; yet, on the other hand, the Calvinist may rightly urge, that, when this constitution of Nature was framed by the Most High, He must have had some plan or purpose concerning it, and that this plan must be worked out, this purpose must be fulfilled. To deny this would be to attribute to the all-wise Creator a degree of providence inferior to that which we must ascribe to every serious and thoughtful man. And yet, who can deny that such a belief carries with it difficulties in regard to the exercise of man's liberty ? We can assert man's liberty as a fact and as the basis of his responsibility, and we shall have the human conscience on our side when we make the assertion. On the other side, we are quite sure that the Divine purpose cannot fail. How these two sets of truths can be brought into accord we cannot tell, and we have no need to make any such attempt, in which it is beyond our powers to succeed. But we may see clearly enough that the opposing schools of theology, perhaps rather of philosophy, have been emphasizing and exaggerating truths which seem to us at variance simply because their reconciliation is beyond our power.

3. When we pass from the study of the

nature and the character of the Most High to the constitution, nature, relations of His creature man, we find that there is here the same want of harmony between those two schools that was shown in regard to the higher subject. When we mention the doctrine of Original Sin, the numerous differences of teaching in regard to man's state and character by nature will occur to us at once; and perhaps we shall be ready to conclude that here we have a chaos of doctrines in which it will be impossible to find any principle of unity. For example, some hold that the Divine image and likeness is entirely lost in man; others, that it is only partially lost; others, that the likeness is lost, but not the image. Some hold that man is totally depraved; others, that he is fallen, but not totally depraved. Some hold that man, without the aid of divine grace, can do the will of God; others, that he is totally unable to do any good thing without help from above; while a great many shades of opinion may be discerned among these leading differences.

We are not concerned to defend the vagaries of individual teachers, so long as we can show that the Church at large has not committed herself to any extreme views on this subject. But we believe that a careful examination even of the extreme theories which have been enunciated on the subject of human depravity will satisfy us that some portion of the difference may be removed by a more careful definition of the terms employed, and still more by taking into account the different points of view of the conflicting theories.

For example, the very nature of original sin is differently defined, — the Church of Rome regarding it as merely negative, the loss of the supernatural gift, wherein, according to their view, the original righteousness of our first parents consisted ; while some other Christian communions regard original sin as something positive. Similarly, there is a difference of definition respecting that natural affection which the English Article[1] calls the φρόνημα σαρκὸς, or concupiscence ; the Article declaring that it has the nature of sin, while the Roman Church declares that it has not the nature of sin. Some, again, declare that children come into the world sinful, while others assert that they are pure and clean.

There are very few subjects, indeed, on which there seems to be a more hopeless diversity of sentiment and judgment; and yet there are very few on which there is a more remarkable fundamental agreement. Let us note some indications of this unity.

In the first place, it will be agreed that the state of nature is not normally a state of grace; and that, although there is a sense in which we may say that a man can do all that he is bound

---

[1] Article IX., "Of Original or Birth Sin."

to do, as the Pelagians said, there is equally a height to which he can aspire, and to which he is bound to aspire when he knows of it, which he can by no means attain without the aid of Divine grace, as the Augustinians declared. Again, it will be conceded by most Christians that there can be no sin, in the proper sense of the word, where there is no conscious transgression of law; yet the nature which we inherit from our parents is not the pure nature which came from the hand of God, and moreover we are actually made subject to the penalties of sins committed by our ancestors before we had any being. The child which dies of a disease resulting from the sin of another is, in no proper sense of the words, guilty of that sin, or punished for that sin; but yet it does bear the penalty which is its consequence. It is very curious to note how, in recent years, science has come to the aid of theology against a shallow view of the nature of man. It is not many years since an English statesman declared that all children came into the world with a soul like a sheet of clean paper. It may be conceded that a certain school of theologians had used unjustifiable language when they spoke of the guilt of little children: there can be no personal guilt where there is no personal offence. But it is satisfactorily established by the research of the scientific students of man's nature, that, instead of coming into the world pure and clean, as some have asserted, we do indeed come with tendencies to all kinds of conduct inherited from the character and constitution of our forefathers. There are few things more remarkable than the way in which thinkers of all schools are coming to an agreement on this subject. Strip the utterances of the contending theologians of their technicalities and their exaggerations, compel them to agree on definitions, to use their terms in the same sense, or at least to understand the sense in which they are used by their antagonists, and their differences will be seen to be so utterly unimportant that we may safely say that there is substantial unity in their teaching.[1]

4. It may seem to some surprising that we should seek for another illustration of this unity of doctrine in the Christian teaching on the subject of Eschatology, the doctrine of the "last things," or of future retribution. This is certainly one of the burning questions of the present day; and although it is now, in a great degree, burnt out, most persons will perhaps hesitate to say that the different opinions prevailing in the Church can be harmonized or reduced to a unity. Let us endeavor to ascertain whether this can be done, although our remarks will necessarily be too much condensed.

On the subject of future retribution three theories have been, more or less, prevalent

[1] See Dr. Bigg's "Christian Platonists," pp. 80, 81, 202, 286. Compare also Poujoulat, "Saint Augustin."

throughout the whole history of the Church: first, that which may be called the Catholic doctrine, although it has been held and taught in various forms,—namely, the doctrine of everlasting punishment; secondly, the doctrine known as Universalism, according to which all men shall be finally saved,—a doctrine which has been taught with a great many degrees of clearness and obscurity; thirdly, the doctrine of annihilation, according to which the finally impenitent will, at some future time, cease to exist, —a doctrine which, in early teaching, so far as we know, was sustained only by the somewhat obscure name of Arnobius,[1] but which, under the name of Conditional Immortality, has obtained considerable acceptance during the past twenty or thirty years.

From the time of the Schoolmen down to the present century, not only has the doctrine of everlasting retribution been taught, but it has been taught in its coarsest and most repulsive form. The imagery employed by the great Italian poet in his "Inferno," is hardly an exaggeration of the popular teaching respecting the sufferings of the lost. It is not too much to say that the doctrine, in this form at least, has been almost abandoned. Yet it can hardly be said

[1] Dr. Pusey ("Everlasting Punishment," p. 195) says the opinion of Arnobius "is obscure, but of no moment." There seems, however, to be no doubt that he taught annihilation. See his work "Adversus Gentes," book ii. chap. 31, 61.

that either of the other theories has taken its place. Universalism, although it may claim to be in accordance with the spirit of much of the teaching of the New Testament regarding the future triumphs of Christ, and the subjection of all things to him, does yet seem so greatly at variance with some distinct teachings in the Gospels and in the Epistles, that it is not held by many who acknowledge either the supreme authority of the Scriptures or the consentient testimony of the Church. The theory of conditional immortality, according to which the finally impenitent will be utterly destroyed and will cease to exist, has certainly no clear authority in the Scriptures, the passages to which appeal is made being, at least, equivocal and uncertain in their meaning; besides which it savors so strongly of materialism, that it is not easily entertained by those who hold the spiritual nature of the human soul. It has been thought, however, — and the notion has a large amount of probability on its side, — that the common doctrine of the Church[1] supplies the elements of truth which are contained in these various theories of future punishment.

In the first place, there can be no doubt that the general teaching of the Church has been in favor of the everlasting duration of the punishment of the finally impenitent. But then the nature of the punishment has never been closely

[1] See Note E.

defined. It might be either of the nature of actual suffering (the *pœna sensus*), or it might be mere privation or loss (the *pœna damni*), without denying that actual suffering might endure for a season. If this last theory be received, as it is now by many thoughtful Christians, we have a doctrine which in a great measure reconciles the various theories. We have a species of Universalism, for actual suffering will in time come to an end; we have a kind of annihilation, for those capacities will be destroyed by which men might rise to the highest privileges of the heavenly life; and there is also a very real kind of everlasting punishment in being deprived of the best blessings of eternity, especially in being forever excluded from the beatific vision.

It would appear — it is at least the judgment of the latest writer on the subject — that something like this was the opinion of Origen.[1] Dr. Bigg, in his Bampton Lectures on the "Christian Platonists of Alexandria," thus interprets the teaching of Origen: "To the Beatific Vision none can be admitted save the pure in heart. Though all other chastisements cease when their object is fulfilled, the *pœna damni* may still endure. Star differeth from star in glory. There are many mansions, many degrees. There

---

[1] The writer has for several years held this view; but it was only in Dr. Bigg's work that he saw it advanced as the doctrine of Origen.

are those who bring forth thirty, sixty, a hundredfold. 'The righteous shall shine as the sun. And upon whom shall they shine but on those beneath them?' If we do not misinterpret these expressions, they appear to mean that the soul by sin may lose capacities which can never be wholly regained; and in this sense, at least, Origen teaches the eternity of punishment."

We are not concerned to prove that men have made no mistakes in their interpretation of the Word of God; nor is any such theory needed to be maintained in order to vindicate the truth and certainty of Scripture doctrine, any more than it is necessary to prove that no mistakes have been made in science before we can believe in the uniformity of the laws of Nature. In truth, the analogy between these two books of God is very close and striking. The book of Nature lies open before us, and we are learning, from age to age, to know more of its secrets and to bring its disclosures into a more perfect harmony. So it is with the book of grace, — the supernatural revelation which God has afforded to mankind, more especially in the person and work of His Incarnate Son, and which He has caused to be written for our learning in Holy Scripture.

That sacred volume has lain open before us for many ages, and men have come with different capacities and with various degrees of preparedness to draw truth from its pages. Many glorious rays of light have, through their labors, been made to shine upon the darkness of our humanity. Some of its rays have been darkened, discolored, perverted by man's ignorance or aversion to the truth. But the process of enlightenment has gone on, although not always without stay or interruption. Dark ages have again and again interrupted the shining light, yet again the darkness has passed away and the true light has shone, and ever its beams have grown brighter and brighter; and so by God's mercy it shall be, until the day break and the shadows flee away, when the night of ignorance and error and partial truth shall have passed forever, and in the beatific vision of Him who is Eternal Truth we behold the perfect day.

LECTURE V.

THE INSUFFICIENCY OF MATERIALISM.

Universality of Belief in God. — Materialism and Atheism inseparably connected. — Materialism, what it is. — Materialistic Accounts of the Origin of Life. — Evolution not necessarily materialistic. — The Atomic Theory no Explanation of Life. — Materialism, pure and simple, generally abandoned. — Opinions of eminent Scientific Men. — The Principle of Energy or Force. — Mr. Spencer's Exposition. — Must we not go further? Mr. Spencer, to some Extent, in Agreement with the Gospel, — but in his "Force" we recognize Mind. — We are compelled to go beyond the Facts and Laws of the Material Universe. — We know Mind directly, Matter indirectly. — What do we learn from the External World? — Kant's Categories. — Laws of Nature imply Mind. — The Argument from Design, — Objections considered. — What we believe and assert. — Our Conclusions called in Question. — Spirit personal. — The Ego and Non-Ego. — The Analogy of the Finite inapplicable to the Infinite. — Conclusions.

"I HAD rather," says Lord Bacon,[1] "believe all the fables in the Legend and the Talmud and the Alcoran, than that this universal frame is without a mind." And it must be confessed that these words represent a sentiment which is well-nigh universal. "It appeareth in nothing more," says the same great writer, "that atheism is rather in the lip than in the heart of

[1] Essay XVI.

man, than by this, that atheists will ever be talking of that their opinion, as if they fainted in it themselves, and would be glad to be strengthened by the consent of others." " What people is there, or what race of men," asks Cicero,[1] "which has not, even without traditional teaching, some notion of the existence of Gods?" The idea seems to be ineradicable. In hours of danger men who have professed unbelief have been heard to call upon the Mightiest for help.

It is well that it should at once be understood that the subject which we have now in hand, Materialism, is inseparably connected with another which is often kept out of sight, Atheism. If there is nothing but matter, then there is no God; if we can know nothing but matter, then we can know nothing of God. We have already attempted to show the insufficiency of atheism, and therefore of materialism, in the life and training of the soul of man. We are now prepared to go further, and maintain that it is insufficient as a theory of the universe. Whether we regard the subject practically or theoretically, we are unable, and we believe that mankind will ultimately be unable, to rest in materialism.

It is not quite easy to say in a few words what is precisely meant by materialism, because, as we shall see, it has assumed different shapes in different hands, — some considering that mat-

[1] De Natura Deorum, i. 16.

ter by itself is sufficient to account for all the phenomena of life, and others postulating a principle which is called Force, or Energy, in addition to matter. We may say generally, however, that materialism has this one characteristic, — that it denies the existence of mind as distinct from matter. It asserts that thought is a product of highly organized matter, and denies that matter and its organization are the work of mind. It maintains that consciousness and personality are not primary facts of existence, but the outcome of the interaction and composition of the elementary particles of matter.

There are various theories with regard to the original form of matter, — some holding what is known as the atomic theory, in one of its various forms; others holding that the primary substance is a fluid which fills all space. Neither of these theories pretends to be more than a mere hypothesis, and therefore they may be safely disregarded in our argument. It is of more importance to consider what account is given of the organization of matter; for it is agreed that matter was once inorganic, and that at some time and in some way organization took place, and life began.

In this respect all purely materialistic systems involve the theories of spontaneous generation and evolution, although these theories are not necessarily connected. To take one example, Dr. Strauss, in his work, already quoted, on

"The Old Faith and the New," considers that, at a certain moment in the past, the cell was spontaneously generated, and so the inorganic became the organic, and in due time life appeared. It is obvious that we are here coming into contact with the scientific theory of evolution, and it is necessary that something should be said on this subject. Briefly we may remark, first, that there is a sense in which evolution may be accepted by a Christian theologian; and, secondly, that the great teacher of evolution, the late Mr. Darwin, never pretended that the theory accounted for life and all existence. He did not deny a creative beginning, — in other words, a God; in the later editions of his book on Species, he refers to a Creator; and so far Christians and theists have no argument with him.[1] As regards the principles of natural selection and the survival of the fittest, many Christians seem to find no difficulty in admitting a large amount of truth in them. For our present purpose, however, it is sufficient to remark that a thorough-going materialist can find no help from Mr. Darwin, and that the advocates of mind and those who teach the existence of a God need have no controversy with him. Dr. Huxley, too, while pointing out that, if evolution, in the whole meaning of the word, be true, "living matter must have arisen from non-living matter," yet admits that there is no

[1] See Note F.

proof of this. "There is not," he says,[1] "a shadow of trustworthy, direct evidence that abiogenesis does take place within the period during which the existence of life on the globe is recorded." Let us, then, endeavor to understand the materialistic solution of the problem of existence, and see whether it will satisfy, not merely the heart and the conscience, but even the demands of the intelligence.

One of the oldest expositions of materialism, pure and simple, is that which is known as the ancient atomic theory. There are many points in this theory, as originally taught, which are open to criticism. For example, the assertion that the atoms differed in size, form, and weight, was utterly irreconcilable with the notion of their indivisibility and ultimate elementary character. As an eminent modern man of science has said,[2] such atoms were evidently "manufactured articles."

But it is not here, principally, that this theory, and every other theory which knows not of anything apart from matter, breaks down hopelessly as an explanation of the origin and formation of the universe as we know it. Suppose we grant or postulate these atoms as the primary forms of matter, or the fluid basis which others prefer, how far have we advanced on the road of explaining the existence of living beings?

---

[1] Art. "Biology," in Encyclopædia Britannica.
[2] Professor Clerk Maxwell.

Suppose we grant the Plenum of the atoms, and the Vacuum, or Void of Space, in what way are these atoms set to work so as to form the combinations of inorganic matter, and then how does this inorganic pass into the organic?

It is unnecessary to give here in detail the answer of the atomists to this question, — the answer, for example, of Democritus, that the atoms fall downwards according to their gravity, and unite according to their homogeneity, or likeness in form and weight, and are guided by the principle of Necessity ($\mathit{ἀνάγκη}$). What is the meaning of "up" and "down" in such circumstances? Such ideas can clearly have no place until Cosmos has emerged from Chaos. And what is the meaning of the Necessity which guides them? The idea of necessity is inseparable from that of law; and law, as we shall see, implies mind, which is utterly excluded by this theory. In short, as has often been pointed out, the Necessity of the atomists is mere Chance ($\mathit{τύχη}$); and this explains nothing. Similar objections may fairly be urged against any other system of materialism, pure and simple; and in consequence, it now finds few, if any, supporters.

This point deserves to be dwelt upon and emphasized. It is lightly assumed by many, who have not taken the pains to acquaint themselves with the state of these controversies, that materialism is a theory which has a good deal to say for itself, which may be true or may be false, but which at any rate demands and deserves consideration, which is opposed chiefly, if not entirely, by theologians and by those who have a prejudice in favor of religion on the one side, or metaphysics on the other.

This assumption is, indeed, very wide of the truth. Lotze is hardly guilty of exaggeration when he says: [1] "The assumption that the common substance of the world is *only matter*, and matter endowed with those properties which we in physical science attribute to every portion of the same, has probably never been made in earnest by any one. Such an assumption would take upon itself the difficult problem of showing how, from these mere properties of space-filling, inertia, divisibility, and mobility, all the rest of the world, and therefore even its spiritual constituents, could be developed as a matter of course, — that is to say, as the mere consequences of such properties, and without admixture of any other principle whatever."

If it should be said that the old atomists had the courage to make this incredible assertion, a slight consideration will show that such a statement would be incorrect. Even Democritus needed the principle of Necessity to account for the movements of the atoms; and modern positivists find it necessary to postulate a very remarkable principle, to the nature of which we shall presently draw attention. In the mean

[1] Philosophy of Religion, chap. ii. § 22.

time let us remind our opponents that the most eminent men in the ranks of science are very far from giving their sanction to the materialistic atheism which now boasts so loudly of its progress.[1]

On this point we will not quote the great names of many who have been sincere Christians as well as ardent students of Nature, from Newton downwards; we can refer to men like Dr. Huxley and Dr. Tyndall, even to Mr. Mill, whose atheistic belief was very much shaken in his later days. Thus, Dr. Huxley[2] remarks: "The materialistic position that there is nothing in the world but matter, force, and necessity, is as utterly devoid of justification as the most baseless of theological dogmas." When Dr. Tyndall was president of the British Association, he was charged with having taught atheism in his inaugural address at Belfast. In the preface to a later edition of his address he gave this answer to the charge: "I have noticed, during years of self-observation, that it is not in hours of clearness and vigor that this doctrine [material atheism] commends itself to my mind; that in the hours of stronger and healthier thought it ever dissolves and disappears, as offering no solution of the mystery in which we dwell."[3] Still stronger are his words in a

[1] See Mr. Cotter Morison's "Service of Man."
[2] Lay Sermons, p. 144.
[3] Belfast Address, Preface to the fifth thousand, p. 36.

subsequent lecture delivered at Manchester, and published along with the Belfast Address: "When standing in the spring-time and looking upon the sprouting foliage, the lilies of the field, and sharing the general joy of opening life, I have often asked myself whether there is no power, being, or thing in the universe, whose knowledge of that of which I am so ignorant is greater than mine. I have asked myself, Can it be possible that man's knowledge is the greatest knowledge, that man's life is the highest life? My friends, the profession of that atheism with which I am sometimes so lightly charged would, in my case, be an impossible answer to the question; only slightly preferable to that fierce and distorted theism which I have lately had reason to know still reigns rampant in some minds, as the survival of a more ferocious age."

In opposition to this disavowal of atheism on the part of Professor Tyndall, it may be pointed out that in the Belfast Address he quotes with approval the words of Lucretius: "Nature is seen to do all things spontaneously of herself without the meddling of the Gods." But it is quite clear that such approval, on his part, was not intended to teach atheism, although it is very likely that Dr. Tyndall holds opinions on the subject of the providence of God which are not consistent with the teaching of Christianity. On the other hand, he may mean no more than a protest against that view of the Divine government which represents the Deity as perpetually interfering in an arbitrary manner with the normal action of cause and effect in Nature and in history. It is not for such a God that we contend. We also believe in a uniformity of Nature. We believe in a God who governs by law and not by caprice, although we should probably differ from some men of science as to the precise sphere of law. With such differences, however, at present we have nothing to do. Our controversy is with materialism; our aim is to show its insufficiency; and so far we have seen that mere materialism has no advocates among men of science. One other quotation may be offered from a writer as distinguished in literature as are those previously named in science. Mr. J. A. Symonds, referring more particularly to the science of evolution, remarks:[1] "Science has not eliminated the conception of a Deity, or effaced the noble humanities secured for us by many centuries of Christian faith. It cannot be too emphatically insisted on that much-dreaded Darwinism leaves the theological belief in a divine spirit untouched. God is not less God, nor is creative energy less creative, because we are led to suppose that a lengthy instead of a sudden method was employed in the production of the Kosmos." It is hardly needful to say that these utterances

[1] Fortnightly Review, June, 1887.

are not here adduced as being authoritative, but only as reasons for hesitating to accept the authoritative statements of a boastful science which disdains to entertain the thought of spirit or God.

Still, it may be said that men of science have professed to explain the phenomena of existence, and to account for the changes and modifications in matter, apart from the action of a personal intelligence; and this they have done by means of the principle which is known under the name of Energy, or Force. These terms have been distinguished; but for our present purpose this is unnecessary.

Among those who seek for an explanation of the universe in matter and force, a prominent place, perhaps the foremost, is held by Mr. Herbert Spencer; and it is to his writings that we must turn for an exposition of the theory. Mr. Spencer says quite truly that "we cannot think at all about the impressions which the external world produces on us, without thinking of them as caused; and we cannot carry out an inquiry concerning their causation, without inevitably committing ourselves to the hypothesis of a First Cause."[1] This first cause, he says, must be finite or infinite. It cannot be finite; but if it is infinite, "we tacitly abandon the hypothesis of causation altogether." This statement we will presently consider. Finally,

[1] First Principles, chap. ii.

THE INSUFFICIENCY OF MATERIALISM. 153

he decides, on grounds which we fully admit, that the First Cause must be infinite and absolute. "These inferences," he says truly, "are forced upon us by arguments from which there appears no escape."[1]

Mr. Spencer then proceeds to show that all religious systems recognize more or less clearly "the omnipresence of something which passes comprehension;" and so he concludes that the "Power which the universe manifests to us is utterly inscrutable."[1] Passing on to details, he shows that "Matter, in its ultimate nature, is as absolutely incomprehensible as Space and Time.[2] . . . Matter is known to us only through its manifestations of Force;" and further, "it is impossible to form any idea of Force in itself," and "it is equally impossible to comprehend its mode of exercise." Repeating the conclusions at which he has arrived, he remarks:[3] "Though the Absolute cannot in any manner or degree be known, in the strict sense of knowing, yet we find that its positive existence is a necessary datum of consciousness; that so long as consciousness continues, we cannot for an instant rid it of this datum; and that thus the belief which this datum constitutes, has a higher warrant than any other whatever."

To this extent Mr. Spencer recognizes the value of religion, that "amidst its many errors

---

[1] First Principles, chap. ii.
[2] Ibid., chap. iii.   [3] Ibid., chap. v.

and corruptions it has asserted and diffused a supreme verity,"— namely, the existence of a "Reality utterly inscrutable in nature." So far we might argue that Mr. Spencer is entirely on our side, at least so far as the negation of mere materialism is concerned. But it is impossible that we should be satisfied with mere negation, and Mr. Spencer will not recognize mind in Nature. Let us see, then, exactly how far he goes, and whether we are not constrained by the necessity of thought to go farther, even to the positive recognition of a Mind in Nature as the only conceivable explanation of its phenomena.

In order to bring out his meaning we will quote two passages,— the first from the sixth chapter, and the second from the fifth chapter, of his "First Principles." "The force," he says, "of which we assert persistence is that Absolute Force of which we are indefinitely conscious as the necessary correlate of the force we know. By the Persistence of Force, we really mean the persistence of some Cause which transcends our knowledge and conception. In asserting it we assert an Unconditioned Reality, without beginning or end." Again, "The consciousness of an Inscrutable Power manifested to us through all phenomena, has been growing ever clearer; and must eventually be freed from its imperfections. The certainty that on the one hand such a Power exists, while on the other hand its nature transcends intuition and is beyond imagination, is the certainty towards which intelligence has from the first been progressing. To this conclusion Science inevitably arrives as it reaches its confines; while to this conclusion Religion is irresistibly driven by criticism. And satisfying as it does the demands of the most rigorous logic, at the same time that it gives the religious sentiment the widest possible sphere of action, it is the conclusion we are bound to accept without reserve or qualification."

Every one can see how near Mr. Spencer's utterances come to the teaching of the Gospel, so near indeed that some have claimed him as a supporter of Divine Revelation. We know, however, that such was not his intention. He meant to declare that the Power which lies behind natural phenomena is both unknown and unknowable. He meant to deny that we had or could have any knowledge of God, if there is a God, and therefore to deny that there is any room for a Divine Revelation. And yet he allows that this hidden power is "manifested," while he says we can know no more of It than is manifested. Now this is, after all, not very different from Christian teaching. We hold that God can be known only in so far as He manifests Himself, and that there are depths in the Divine nature which man cannot explore.

There is, however, one postulate in our statements which Mr. Spencer would not concede. In the Power, the Force which lies behind the phenomena of Nature, we recognize Mind, we discover a Person; and this to Mr. Spencer would be a contradiction. It is necessary, therefore, that we should point out the insufficiency and unsatisfactoriness of the positivist and agnostic position generally, and also indicate the steps by which we arrive at the conclusion to which we hold fast. In doing so, we set ourselves in opposition not to Mr. Spencer or any other writer in particular, nor to any particular form of materialism, but to that system in general which refuses to consider any truths as ascertained beyond the facts and laws of the material universe, which denies that behind the phenomena of nature we can recognize an Infinite Mind, a Personal God. In other words, we here break away from the agnostic position generally.

Now, let us consider what statements like those of the Positivist or Agnostic actually mean and imply. Certainly, there is this involved in them, — that we may know matter, but that we cannot know mind; or else that while matter exists and may be known, there really is no mind for us to know. As has already been said, according to the system which we are opposing, thought is a mere product of organized matter, generated as, for example, electricity is generated, and needs nothing else to account for it but the interaction of material particles.

We do not at present ask if such a system can

satisfy our conscience, our religious nature, our longings for immortality, and the like. We now ask merely whether it will satisfy our intelligence. Having regard to what we know of ourselves, can we believe it? It would hardly be possible, we imagine, to give a better answer to this theory which tells us that we can know matter but that we cannot know mind, than that which is given by Lotze in his " Mikrokosmus."[1] "Among all the errors of the human mind," he remarks, "it has always seemed to me the strangest that it could come to doubt its own existence, of which alone it has direct experience, or to take it at second hand as the product of an external Nature which we know only indirectly, — only by means of the knowledge of the very mind to which we would deny existence."

Thoroughly to understand this statement is unhesitatingly to receive it as true. We do not really know the external world. We know, directly and immediately, only our own states of mind. "We are so used in Nature," says Lotze again, "to find momentous differences in properties traced back to trifling alterations in the amount and mode of combination of homogeneous elements, that at last we lose all understanding of anything immediate, and unconsciously become possessed by a passion for construing everything, assigning to everything a complicated machinery as the means of its origination and

[1] Book ii. chap. v. p. 263 (English translation).

operation. We would then fain assert that even within us there is nothing but an exterior concatenation of events, resembling the communication of movement by which, in the outer world, we see one element come into collision with another; and all else that we find within, — consciousness, feeling, and effort, — we are almost tempted to regard as only a kind of accidental reflection in us of that real action, unless indeed we see that there must be something for which and in which this reflection arises. That something there is; every several expression of our consciousness, every stirring of our feelings, every dawning resolution, calls aloud that processes, not to be measured by the standard of physical notions, do indeed take place with unconquerable and undeniable reality. So long as we have this experience," the writer goes on, "Materialism may prolong its existence and celebrate its triumphs within the schools, where so many ideas estranged from life take shelter; but its own professors will belie their false creed in their living action. For they will all continue to love and hate, to hope and fear, to dream and study; and they will in vain seek to persuade us that this varied exercise of mental energies, which even deliberate denial of the supersensual cannot destroy, is a product of their bodily organization, or that the love of truth exhibited by some, the sensitive vanity betrayed by others, has its origin in their cerebral fibres."

So far, then, we maintain that mind is not a thing to us unknown, or a thing which we know through the medium of matter: we maintain, on the contrary, that we know mind directly and immediately, and matter only through the medium of mind. And this leads us to ask what is the nature of the knowledge which we have of the external world, — whether the thoughtful study of its phenomena will guide us to an acquiescence in the opinion that there is nothing which can be known in Nature save matter and an unknown and unknowable force which works in it, or whether we shall not be constrained to recognize behind the phenomena of Nature the existence of a Personal Mind, which, although It be infinite and absolute, and therefore such as cannot be comprehended by the finite and the relative, yet may be, and actually is, known in so far as It reveals Itself and as that revelation is received by man. It seems to us that this latter conclusion may be "demonstrated" with sufficient completeness, having regard to the nature of the subject.

It was one chief aim of the philosopher Kant, in his "Critique of Pure Reason," to point out that there was a necessary *a priori* element in the mind of man, without which no experience would be possible. Kant did not for a moment think of denying that all our knowledge came to us through experience, through sensuous experience; but he pointed out that before our sensations could be turned into thoughts there must be an operation of elements not given from without, but already existing in the mind itself. This is, in brief, Kant's doctrine of the categories, or forms of thought in the understanding. A simple illustration of this doctrine will lead us on our way to the goal which we are endeavoring to reach.

When we turn our eyes towards external objects, we first note certain resemblances or differences by which they are distinguished. We proceed to generalize and classify, and to note the relations which subsist between one object and another, between ourselves and those objects of our perceptions. Our knowledge or observation of those relations is set forth in what we call a law; and so by degrees we come to a knowledge of the laws of Nature, — the law of gravitation, for example, the laws under which matter expands and contracts, and the like. Whence do we obtain the knowledge of those laws? Not from mere sensation. Mere sensation has not the character of thought. The element by which that is constituted must be derived from the mind itself. It is this which principally distinguishes man from the lower species of animated Nature. There is, then, a sense in which laws are made by man. And at this point the argument is sometimes allowed to stop; but surely the same train of reasoning may be carried further.

When we speak of laws of Nature which are perceived by all men in common who are endowed with the same nature as ourselves, we do not mean that we have invented or created those laws. It is true, they are not present in our sensations. They do not present themselves visibly or tangibly to our perception. We cannot in any way make an image or picture of them. They are inferences of the mind from the phenomena of Nature. But, although inferences of the mind, they are not creations of the mind. They have a certain kind of existence, for they are actually operating. Where, then, do they exist? There can be but one answer to that question. They exist in a Mind which bears a certain resemblance to our own. And this, in fact, it is, which makes it possible for ourselves to recognize them. The mind of man perceives in Nature the working of a mind to which it is itself akin.

This argument is quite distinct, as you will readily perceive, from the so-called teleological, or argument from design. As, however, we believe that this latter argument is valid, although we do not rest upon it, and as both arguments have certain objections urged against them in common, we will here briefly indicate the nature of the argument from design, variously known as the argument from final causes, the teleological, or the physico-theological argument.

It is certainly one of our deepest convictions,

that everything which exists has some use or purpose; and we can generally trace the appearance of design in the objects of Nature. Even Mr. Herbert Spencer declares that "there can be no true conception of a structure without a true conception of its function. To understand how an organization originated and developed, it is requisite to understand the need subserved."[1] This sounds very much like teleology. Now, it may be quite true that Kant's metaphysical objections to this argument are unanswerable; and yet it may not follow that it has not a certain amount of validity. In fact, there are few persons who can entirely divest themselves of a feeling of its power. It is the most popular of all the theories. Even Kant had a tenderness for it. It came very near freeing J. S. Mill from the bondage of atheism. We may even hope that it succeeded. When a man can write, as Mr. Mill wrote,[2] "It must be allowed that, in the present state of our knowledge, the adaptations in Nature afford a large balance of probability in favor of creation by intelligence," he cannot be far from the faith of the Unseen. A large balance of probability? Surely, this is practical demonstration; for, as Butler remarks, "to us probability is the very guide of life."

It is objected, however, by Mill, Kant, and others, that even if we accepted all that is

---

[1] Ecclesiastical Institutions, chap. i.
[2] Three Essays, p. 174.

fairly deducible from the appearance of purpose in the world, the result would be insufficient. We should have the revelation of a finite and limited being, and not of One who was infinite and absolute. Let us see how far such an objection is valid. Kant states it in the following manner: "The utmost," he says,[1] "that could be established by such a proof would be an *Architect of the world*, always very much hampered by the quality of the material with which he has to work, not a *Creator*, to whose idea everything is subject. This would by no means suffice for the purposed aim of proving an all-sufficient original Being." Somewhat to the same effect are the remarks of Mr. Mill. He says the argument from design proves a Former, and not a Creator, and that it does not prove the Maker to be infinite or all-powerful.

Now, what is the real value of these objections? Do they not simply tell us that the Infinite cannot or does not reveal His infinity? But how is it possible that He should do so? For in that case He must first have created another Infinite to whom He could be revealed. And such a notion is a simple contradiction. There cannot be two Infinites, two Absolutes, two universes. In creation the Creator of necessity imposes limitations upon Himself in doing His

[1] Critique of Pure Reason, part ii., division ii., p. 538 (Max Müller's translation).

work; and in this there is nothing derogatory to His glory and greatness. The limitation is from within, and not from without.

A similar answer must be given to the objection that the Mind which we recognize behind or under Nature in the laws by which it is governed is not an Infinite Mind, or at least is not known as such. It will be necessary to state very carefully what we actually maintain, before we proceed to meet the various objections as they arise. In the first place, then, we hold that there is in Nature a revelation of Mind, and on this point perhaps enough has been said. Further, we are agreed with our opponents that an Infinite Mind is not, and cannot, be revealed in creation. But, again, we maintain that there is an Infinite and Absolute, the Origin, Basis, Condition of all existence. Further, that this Absolute is Intelligence, Mind, Thought, Spirit. Moreover, that this Spirit is personal; and finally, that the belief in the personality of the Infinite and Absolute involves no contradiction whatever. If we can satisfactorily establish these points, our work will be accomplished.

We have already pointed out that the cause or ground, whichever you please,[1] of those natural phenomena in which we discern the operation of law must be mental, spiritual; and we have admitted that we have no demonstration of the

[1] We do not stand out for the word "cause;" "ground," "basis," "origin," will do quite as well.

infinitude of that cause. But it is quite clear[1] that the First Cause must be infinite; for if it is finite, limited, then we must think of something beyond its limits, so that there is something else which must be taken into account in estimating the complete nature of the First Cause, or else we must believe in something existing which has not been caused; and if this is admitted we must allow that there is no need to assume a cause for anything, so that the principle of causation must be given up. It is, therefore, impossible that the First Cause should be other than infinite.

So, again, the First Cause must be independent. "If it is dependent, it cannot be the First Cause; for that must be the First Cause on which it depends. . . . Thus the First Cause must be in every sense perfect, complete, total, including within itself all power; or, to use the established word, it must be absolute." It would detain us too long to repeat here the criticism of these statements offered by Mr. Spencer and others, especially as we are not resting our argument upon them. The conclusion at which we arrive is well stated, although it is not accepted, by Mr. Spencer. "Here, then," he says, "respecting the nature of the universe, we seem committed to certain unavoidable conclusions. The objects and actions surrounding us, not less

[1] Compare the statement in Spencer's "First Principles," chap. ii.

than the phenomena of our own consciousness, compel us to ask a cause; in our search for a cause we discover no resting-place until we arrive at the hypothesis of a First Cause; and we have no alternative but to regard this First as infinite and absolute."

May we not, then, conclude, in view of the decision already arrived at, that the existence of Mind is required to explain the phenomena of Nature, and that we must think of the First Cause as Infinite Mind? So it would appear. For, if not, we must at any rate say that the immediate cause of phenomena is a mind, even if we cannot deny that that mind itself may have been caused. But if this is so, then the more remote cause must also have been a mind, and so on until we reach the First Cause, which itself must also be a mind, and infinite and independent; so that again we reach the idea of Absolute Mind as the First Cause.

However just this reasoning may appear, it is called in question from various quarters. In the first place, we are reminded of Hegel's theory of the absolute as Spirit, which comes to consciousness in man; and secondly, we are told that Personality and the Absolute are incompatible ideas, — that the Infinite is, of necessity, impersonal, and personality is, of necessity, finite. Let us examine these statements. In the previous remarks we were dealing with a scientific objection. Here we are met by a metaphysical.

When Hegel declares that the Absolute is Spirit, and that the Spirit attains to consciousness in man, he certainly seems to teach the impersonality of the Absolute, — in other words, sheer pantheism. It is quite true that the most eminent expounder of Hegelian doctrine in the English language, Dr. Stirling, asserts that Hegel was no pantheist, and that he did not mean to teach pantheistic doctrine. It is, perhaps, a bold thing to say positively what Hegel must have meant. Certainly, he has very commonly been understood to teach pantheism, and it is difficult to attach any other meaning to his words.[1] But in any case we must consider the difficulty, and see whether it involves any real objection to our conclusion respecting the cause of the universe.

The views, then, to which we refer, "commonly announce this element [the Absolute] as a Reason which is *per se* unconscious; which only in individual points of its extreme altitude, in individual spiritual beings, raises itself to consciousness."[2] This view is well answered by Lotze, who says: " Such a form of conception as the foregoing appears inadmissible. We have no right to strip off from the Reason which we invariably first learn by experience to know as conscious, this predicate of consciousness, and then

---

[1] Dr. Morris, the accomplished Professor of Philosophy in the University of Michigan, has drawn my attention to passages in Hegel which support Dr. Stirling's view.

[2] Lotze, "Philosophy of Religion," chap. ii. § 24.

persuade ourselves that aught intelligible is left still remaining. Rather is it true that only one definite thought admits of being connected with the expression, 'a reason acting unconsciously in the world;' namely, the thought that *blind* forces act in the world, which are not in any respect reason, but which in fact act so that their results are the same as those which a reason acting in the world would have been compelled to desire."

If we declare that such a conclusion is at variance with all experience, we shall probably be told that we have no right to infer anything concerning the infinite from what we know of the finite. But we must remind the objector that we are here keeping strictly within the limits of that which we do know, — namely, mind and its operations. We do know our own mind directly and immediately, and by that mind we are compelled to recognize the working of mind in the phenomena of Nature.

It is only another way of stating the same view which we have just mentioned, when we are told that the Absolute is Spirit, but *impersonal* Spirit. Here, again, we give in substance the answer of Lotze. It is easy enough to employ phrases of this kind, but it is difficult, it is impossible, to attach any intelligible meaning to them. It is quite true that we are not always, so to speak, conscious of personality. We experience many states of feeling in which all attention is withdrawn from our own self, and we do not think of ourselves as distinct from the non-self of the external world. The sensation, the feeling, the notion, the effort, is for the time everything, and we ourselves, as the subjects of those states, are forgotten.

Granting all this, it is equally clear that these states are all facts which take place in a personal spirit. "They merely prove that it is not necessary for the personal spirit at every moment to think of itself as different from the content which exactly fills out its consciousness. But they cannot prove that anything similar is possible without the personality, which, in such a case, does not indeed mentally represent itself, but none the less remains in fact the condition of the possibility of such a self-forgetfulness. For all the aforesaid sensations, ideas, or feelings, in which we thus lose ourselves, are, after all, never thinkable except as states of a definite, self-identical, and distinct spiritual subject, and not the least consecutiveness, nor any coherency according to law between these different spiritual states, would be possible, unless the personal unity of the Spirit, which is by no means apparent in them, were, for all that, the real ground which unites them with one another."

One other statement, drawn from the nature of Personality, remains to be considered. It is alleged that the idea of Personality is incompatible with that of the Absolute. The Ego, it is said, cannot be thought without a Non-Ego. The moment we say *I*, we imply a something which is *Not-I;* and such a contrast is impossible to the Absolute, which is infinite and all-comprehending. By attributing to the Absolute such an attribute, it is said, we make Him finite. It is important to examine this objection, since we must probably regard it as the principal argument now commonly employed to destroy the proof of the Divine Personality. How far is it valid, or the reverse? Let us grant, then, that in thinking of our own personality, in calling one's self *I*, we do mark out our own position as distinct from that of the world around us, or whatever it may be, perhaps we should say rather the whole of existence besides ourselves, which we call the Non-Ego. This is quite clear. Yet this Non-Ego, this negative conception, is not the idea in which the sense of our own personality originated. On the contrary, personal existence is implied in all mental experience. Every feeling and thought and effort supposes a ground in which it has its origin, a ground in which consciousness exists altogether apart from any consideration of its external relations. It is when the Ego looks upon itself as limited, when it becomes conscious of its limitations, that it recognizes outside of itself all that is not contained within those limitations; and this is what it distinguishes from itself as the not-self, or Non-Ego.

But surely these very considerations show how inapplicable are these limitations to the Absolute; for He is the absolutely unconditioned. It is because we are forced to acknowledge our own limitations that we are compelled to recognize a Non-ego or Not-I. We can draw a circular line around ourselves, and outside of that circle, limited as it is, there is the unlimited. But the Absolute and the Infinite cannot be thus enclosed, and there is no finite or infinite external to Him. By whatever name we call this Absolute, we can say, " Of Him, and through Him, and to Him, and in Him are all things;" yea, in the Absolute " we live and move and have our being." [1]

From another point of view it is clear that the analogy of the finite is inapplicable to the Infinite. It is by means of the external world that the finite is roused to feeling, thought, and action; and in this respect the Non-Ego plays a part which can have nothing corresponding to it in the nature of the Infinite,— for that is absolutely self-sufficient, and is dependent upon nothing besides itself.

Let us see, then, to what our inquiry has conducted us. We set out with the thesis of the insufficiency of materialism, and we have done our best to consider what has been, and can be,

---

[1] The Christian doctrine of the Trinity will suggest itself as meeting some of the difficulties proposed. But it could not properly be here used as an argument.

urged on the other side. It is true that our treatment of the subject has been very partial and incomplete. It could not be otherwise. Apart from the limitations of time, it would not be possible or expedient to enter upon a prolonged metaphysical discussion. But no difficulty of importance has been ignored; and it is believed that the answers which have been suggested in outline will bear the test of examination, and will acquire additional force the longer they are considered.

What, then, are the conclusions at which we have arrived? And are they such as to justify us in pronouncing upon the insufficiency of materialism? We have shown that materialism, pure and simple, is now held by no school of thought, — that the notion that all existence has originated from certain elementary particles of matter and their interaction, is abandoned by all scientific thinkers as an impossible theory of the world. We have seen that many, endeavoring to supply the defects of a merely materialistic theory, have supposed the existence of another principle which is called Force or Energy, — a power which certainly acts and is manifested in the phenomena of the world, yet which is unknown and unknowable. We have recognized in this energy some of the attributes which we are accustomed to apply to Almighty God; but while we acknowledge that He is in a sense the unknowable, the unsearchable, yet we declare that He has manifested Himself to man in various ways, and that by such manifestation He has made Himself known. Further, we attempted to show that this Power or Force, behind Nature or beneath it, — the World-cause, the World-ground, the World-order, as it has been differently named, — must be Mind. For in examining the phenomena of Nature, or the World, we discern beneath the distinct effects the operation of principles, which we call by the name of laws, in which laws we recognize the working of a Mind to which our own is akin.[1]

At this point we paused to consider some theories of a different character, and some objections to the personality of the Absolute Mind whom we recognized as the ground of existence. On the one hand, we saw that there was no ground for holding that the undeveloped Spirit was unconscious as an inference from similar states in the case of finite beings; on the other, that the expression Impersonal Spirit was a mere phrase, to which no intelligible meaning could be attached. Further, the argument that the assertion of personality was the denial of the absolute was shown to rest upon an imperfect examination of finite experience, and, even if it were valid for the finite, could have no application to the Infinite.

[1] This conclusion, scientifically deduced, falls in with the teaching of Divine Revelation, that man is made in the image of God.

It is sometimes said that the arguments of the Christian Apologist are drawn from sources with which the man of science cannot deal,— from feeling, faith, authority, personal experience, and the like. He will not, perhaps, be a wise guide of humanity who will ignore elements which constitute so large a portion of human life and action. But, so far, we have listened to no arguments but those which are derived from reason. If they are not allowed to be of a kind which we have a right to employ, then we can only say that all knowledge, all certainty, becomes impossible, and we are involved in a universal scepticism.

When Bishop Berkeley denied the independent existence of the external world, he was supposed to destroy the grounds of belief and action, and to lead to scepticism. As a matter of fact, he intended to strengthen those grounds, and, rightly understood, he certainly did not weaken them. When our modern materialists tell us that we know nothing except matter and its laws, they do in fact destroy the very grounds of knowledge and of certainty. They declare our ignorance of that through which alone we can know anything at all. If there is any knowledge, there is the knowledge of mind; and if we have the knowledge of mind, then we cannot stop short of recognizing the mind which works in what we call the laws of Nature.

We are contented with this line of argument,

and we believe it is conclusive; but we are not contented to ignore other elements in man's constitution. When we spoke of the true nature of a full and liberal human culture, we attempted to show how insufficient was every provision for that purpose which did not include the knowledge of God. The thought might be carried further. We might apply it to the facts of human history and human experience in all the extent of their significance.

Man is a worshipper. He has always worshipped. He cannot help worshipping. If he cannot find God, he will fashion an idol and fall down before the work of his hands. And what does materialistic science offer him in place of God? An absolute, unknown, and unknowable Force. Can he worship thus: —

"We praise Thee, O Eternal Force: we acknowledge Thee to be unsearchable.
All the earth doth worship Thee, the Absolute, the Unknowable"?

How, we must ask again, will it help the conscience and the will to be told to fall in with the "stream of tendency that makes for righteousness," or to cultivate "a morality touched with emotion"?

But there is something darker and deadlier still to remember as the outcome of this degrading theory which turns life into death, and shuts the gates of immortality before the longing eyes of us poor children of a day. It is not merely, as has already been pointed out, that it takes away one great motive for moral effort, and changes the whole character of man's life and work on earth. There is something involved in it even worse than this. It is the destruction of the hope in which is rooted a chief part of the joy of living. It is the brooding of that hopelessness over the family of man which results, and necessarily results, in the dark despair of pessimism, the most blighting faith or unfaith that the world has ever known.

God is the necessary and universal postulate of all human life and thought and action. He is the ground of all our knowledge; for all thought becomes confused when He is banished or ignored. He is the root of the moral nature, the conscience, the will; for right and wrong have no real meaning if there is no God, and the conscience is left to struggle with the perplexity caused by a voice speaking with authority from within, which yet can give no account of any lawful source from which it derives its sanctions. No one pretends that the "hypothesis of God" explains all the mysteries or removes all the difficulties which are found in human history. But it does at least help to introduce something like unity into the multiplicity of movements, mental and physical, in which we have our own place and action; even if it also brings us face to face with other difficulties which do not emerge in a system which knows no God.

Yes, it must be admitted that the existence of a personal God does involve difficulties in view of the actual condition of the world and man. But here, again, we have a way of escape and a door of hope opened to us. If we knew only of the God who is revealed to us in Nature and in history, we should indeed be perplexed and doubtful and anxious in regard to our own destiny, and that of our fellow-men. But the existence of a personal God may well suggest to us the possibility of some higher disclosure of His mind than that which is found in the natural order.

And what is there to hinder our belief in such a revelation? A freethinking deistical writer some years ago attempted to pour derision upon what he called contemptuously a Book Revelation, asserting that God did sufficiently reveal Himself in the heart and life of man, and that no other revelation was necessary or credible.

Whether any further revelation is necessary is a question which is sufficiently answered, one might suppose, by the nations of the world who make no claim to possess such revelation. No one will pretend that in any place or time men stand in no need of further illumination. Nor is it strictly accurate to speak of the Christian system as a Book Revelation. God was manifest in the flesh. It was a revelation, in its highest form and expression, in a human life.

And if it be said that we are here entering boldly into the region of what is called "supernatural religion," we reply that there is no other religion but the supernatural; for religion has to do with God, and God is above Nature. And he who believes in a personal God may well believe that He will reveal Himself to His creatures.

On this point, happily, there is now little dispute. If there is no God, of course a miracle is inconceivable. If we are to accept the pantheistic theory, which is only materialism or atheism in another form, then too a miracle is as little to be thought of. But if the world is ruled and governed by an intelligent, conscious, voluntary Being, who knows His creatures and can hold communion with them, then miracles — supernatural testimonies to the presence, mind, working, of God among men — are neither impossible nor improbable.

Such a revelation, such a supernatural manifestation of Himself, we believe that God has given, communicating to mankind thereby a knowledge of Himself so high, so pure, so full, that in comparison with it all other knowledge is but ignorance. "No man knoweth the Father but the Son, and he to whom the Son will reveal Him." Blessed are our eyes, for they see this glorious manifestation of the Most High God. Blessed are our ears, for they hear the message of love and mercy which comes to us from the lips of the Crucified, the Raised, the Glorified. May our hearts be opened to receive His grace! May we never turn a deaf ear to His offers! "Lord, to whom shall we go? Thou hast the words of eternal life."

LECTURE VI.

THE PESSIMISM OF THE AGE.

Connection between Faith and Action. — Different Tendencies in Human Nature explain the Origin of Pessimism and Optimism. — Meaning of these Terms. — Views of Jews, Greeks, and Romans. — Christian View. — Sentiment of Deism. — Buddhism. — I. Modern Pessimism, — Leopardi, Schopenhauer, Hartmann; Leopardi's three possible Ways of Happiness; Schopenhauer's Theory. — II. What we are to think of Pessimism. — 1. Effort not necessarily productive of Unhappiness; 2. Pleasure not merely Negative; 3. The Development and Elevation of Life not a mere Increase of Misery. — Increased Sensibility and Intelligence also a Source of Happiness. — Testimonies of Instinct and Reason. — The Reply of Pessimism: Men deceive themselves. — The Rejoinder of Consciousness. — A Future Life. — III. How can we account for Pessimism? — Partly the Result of Temperament and Constitution, partly of the Circumstances of Individuals and Communities. — Chief Cause found in the State of Religious Belief. — Condition of Germany. — Pessimism can flourish only on the Ruins of Faith. — Examples of Faith and Unbelief. — The Gospel and Agnosticism. — Deism. — Atheism. — Pessimism the last Word of Positivism. — Conclusion.

A WRITER, to some of whose theories attention will be given in the present lecture, has declared that a man's faith cannot be wrong if his life is right.

"For forms of faith let graceless bigots fight;
His can't be wrong whose life is in the right."

And some have gone still further, and have professed to regard all beliefs as unimportant, as having no necessary effect upon conduct. A man may be an atheist or a Christian, they argue; but this need make no difference in the principles by which he guides his life. Belief in a Supreme Being or in the Christian religion is not necessary in order to a well-ordered manner of living.

Whatever allowance may have to be made for the inconsistencies of professing Christians, we are confident that no one who really examines with any care the consequences of faith and unbelief in human history will consider these conclusions to be tenable. On the contrary, we shall find the whole social system of particular countries and localities colored by the dominant religious belief; we shall find particular ages and epochs of the world profoundly affected by the theological and metaphysical opinions which had chief influence in those periods. It is because we entertain this conviction, and particularly because we believe the disease of pessimism[1] to be a malady of the present day, produced by the peculiar character of the prevalent form of unbelief, that we have chosen it as a

[1] On this subject M. Caro published an interesting set of papers in the "Revue des Deux Mondes," which were afterwards collected and published in one volume. I am sorry that I was unable to procure Mr. Sully's work on Pessimism, as it was out of print.

subject to be discussed in the present series of lectures.

We shall find some explanation of the origin of pessimism and of its opposite in the different tendencies of human nature which are visible, more or less, in every era of its history, — the tendency, on the one hand, to make the best of everything, and the opposite tendency to make the worst of everything. These tendencies seem to arise from various causes; to be generated, in fact, sometimes by natural constitution and temperament, sometimes by the state of a man's health, sometimes by the favorable or adverse circumstances in which he is placed. They produce different theories of human life, — theories which are modified in various ways, but which may be generally described as the theories of Optimism and Pessimism.

When a man says he is an optimist, he means either that everything is actually as good as it can be, — and this is the extreme form of the theory; or else that everything is working out a result which on the whole will be the best possible, — and this is perhaps the more ordinary form. When a man says he is a pessimist, he means that everything is very bad, — not perhaps the worst that can be, for then it could be no worse, and he holds that things are growing worse and worse; but that mere existence is an evil, and that any good which may be connected with it does not constitute its main character, but is simply a slight alleviation of its general misery, some feeble streaks of light breaking the monotony of its gloom.

The general belief of the ancients — Jews, Greeks, and Romans — was a species of optimism. They believed that man was made for happiness; and further, they believed that men might be happy and were happy unless this natural result were hindered by some adverse power. The Jew had for his possession a land flowing with milk and honey. He had the promise that he should eat the good of the land, and sit in peace " under the vine and under the fig-tree." If it were otherwise with him, it was because he had fallen away from the God of Israel.

The Greek and the Roman had the same conviction that his normal condition was one of enjoyment. If he suffered in mind, body, or estate, it was through the action of some offended deity whom he must propitiate, or through the influence of some envious or malicious being whom he must reconcile or appease. In the optimism of the ancients, as perhaps we must say in all unmitigated optimism,[1] there is a degree of one-sidedness and shallowness. Even if in its main principle it is right, it excludes or ignores a considerable portion of the facts of man's life; it takes no account of its darker aspects, which, nevertheless, are as real as its brighter. One

[1] See Hartmann's remarks, quoted in Note G.

feels keenly the wide separation, in this respect, between Paganism and Christianity. The pagan ideal is the Apollo, radiant with health and strength and beauty and hope. The Christian ideal is the Man of sorrows, acquainted with grief, His face marred more than any man's. There can be no doubt that the Christian ideal is the truer, the deeper, the more tender, and that which exercises the most powerful influence over the heart and mind of man.

It would be a strange, an inexcusable mistake, however, to suppose that the Gospel, even in its saddest aspects, encourages the theory of pessimism. The cross is but the way to the crown. Christianity cannot, and will not, ignore the facts of human life, — its sinfulness, guilt, and misery. Where sin is, there must be suffering. The penalty lies upon the sinful individual, upon the sinful race. All have sinned, and all must suffer, — most of all, that One who answers for all who partake of that nature which He has assumed ; but, with the Gospel, this suffering is transitional. "Weeping may endure for a night, but joy cometh in the morning." Those who come weeping to the grave find it empty; those who ask after the buried Master are seeking for the living among the dead. He is not there; He is risen.

Consequently, all true Christian philosophy, although it has never overlooked the terrible character and effects of sin, has ever spoken of man's destiny in a hopeful tone. Even the more pensive spirits, the Augustines and the Pascals, who sometimes seem almost to revel in their melancholy, never regard evil as a *necessity*, as a *law*, and therefore never approximate to pessimism. Human sin and misery, in their judgment, is the result of alienation from God, and is to be healed by reconciliation to God. Man is to be restored by grace. In the Gospel the element of hope separates it off absolutely and entirely from pessimism, which is simply the doctrine of despair.

Christian philosophy must always, then, in its prevailing tone be optimist; and the same may be said of every philosophy which believes in a personal God. Such was the prevailing tone of thought with all classes of thinkers in the eighteenth century. Believers, sceptics, unbelievers alike, — most of the last were deists, and not atheists, — were optimists, and generally of a very pronounced kind. Many of them held not merely that a good time was coming, that all things were *working* for good, but that all things *were* good. "Whatever is, is right;" and this aphorism they sometimes charged with a meaning which was certainly not Christian.

To this school, generally, belonged the poet Pope; the freethinkers Voltaire and Rousseau, with slight differences of opinion in detail; and, to a great extent, the illustrious Christian apologist Paley. The most eminent philosophical expounder of optimism was Leibnitz, who in his "Théodicée" declared that "the world, as it is, is the best of all possible worlds." This is the doctrine of Pope in his " Essay on Man:"—

> "All nature is but art, unknown to thee;
> All chance, direction which thou canst not see;
> All discord, harmony not understood;
> All partial evil, universal good;
> And spite of pride, in erring reason's spite,
> One truth is clear, Whatever is, is right."

Statements so broad were susceptible of many explanations, and might be true or false as they were understood. To those who believe in moral good or evil, in right and wrong, many things are which are not right, — that is to say, *absolutely* and in themselves right; to those who believe in a personal God, who is Creator, Preserver, Ruler, Benefactor, Lover of all, there is a sense in which all is and must be *relatively* right, — in such a sense, we mean, that, on the whole, it is better that things should be as they are than that they should not be ; that, on the whole, creation and existence will prove not to have been an evil, but a good, for the manifestation of the glory of the Creator in the securing of good for the created.

Even Rousseau could see that some such principles as these must constitute the belief of theists. "The true principles of optimists," he says, "can be deduced neither from the properties of matter nor from the mechanism of the universe, but only from the perfections of God, who presides over all; so that the existence of God is not proved by the system of Pope, but the system of Pope by the existence of God."

We have spoken of the ancient nations of the West and of the Hebrews as being optimist. Farther east we come into contact with a different tendency, which finds its extreme expression in Buddhism. According to this religion, if it can be called a religion, *existence is the great evil;* and everything which tends to increase the sum of conscious being is to be discouraged and resisted. It is desire which produces existence. Desire is born of the perception of the illusory forms of being; and these are so many effects of ignorance. It is ignorance, therefore, which is the first cause of all that seems to exist. To know this ignorance is, at the same time, to destroy its effects. The supreme knowledge for man, then, is the ceasing to deceive himself. It is, at the same time, the supreme deliverance, which has *four degrees*, successively passed through by the dying Buddha: (1) To know the nature and the vanity of all things; (2) To destroy in one's self judgment and reason; (3) To attain to absolute indifference; (4) Finally, to annihilate all pleasure, all memory, all consciousness. This is the state known as *Nirvâna*, in which every light is extinguished, every idea is gone;

in which, as has been well said, there is neither idea nor absence of ideas, there is nothing. Modern pessimism bears the closest possible resemblance to Buddhism. It starts from the same origin, — the absolute worthlessness of human life and of all existence; it seeks the same end, — the total extinction of desire, of feeling, of all conscious existence. It is *an evil to be*, — the higher the degree of existence, the greater the evil; therefore the highest good is that being should cease. It is contended by some that *Nirvâna* does not involve annihilation. To a Western mind, at least, the difference is unintelligible and inconceivable.

I. The first apostle of modern pessimism was the Italian poet Leopardi. He was a man of noble birth, apparently of spotless life, and endowed with many estimable qualities. But his bodily health was weak, — he was through life a great sufferer, — he was disappointed of some of his dearest hopes, and he fell under the influence of a monk who had apostatized from the Christian faith. Although Leopardi seems to have died with some kind of belief, seeing that he received the last offices of the Church, it is evident that through life he was entirely destitute of anything that could properly be called faith in Christ or in God. Morbid, suffering, disappointed, disbelieving, his only refuge was a philosophy of despair. Although his German fellow-laborer in the same cause,

Schopenhauer, began his work about the same time, seventy years ago (1818), Leopardi was the first to become widely known, and to diffuse the theories which are now most closely associated with the name of Schopenhauer.

Leopardi, like Sakya Mouni, the founder of Buddhism, held that the great evil was existence. But he and, in a greater degree, his successors have given a scientific form to a theory which, with the Oriental mystic, was like an intuitive conviction, and not a reasoned belief. "All," says Leopardi, "is a secret, except our sorrow."[1] "Our life," he says again, — "what is its worth, except to be despised?"[2] And this, which was his own deepest conviction, he seeks to demonstrate by an examination of the various possible sources of happiness.

There are, it is said, three conceivable ways of happiness: it may be found in the world as it is; it may be looked for in the world to come; it may be labored for and prepared on behalf of future generations when the world shall be better than it is now. These statements are very general. A Christian would refuse to have these sources of happiness separated; he would insist on blending them, instead of relying upon any one of them by itself. But the pessimist is quite right in saying that, if there

---

[1] "Arcano è tutto
Fuor che il nostro dolor."
[2] "Nostra vita a che val! Solo a spregiarla."

is no reality in the happiness promised by any one of these ways, then the hope of happiness is a delusion.

Leopardi sets to work to show that none of these ways of happiness has any reality. (1) As regards the present, he says he has tried it and found it empty. The last illusion is gone, he says. Hope has left him; even desire is stilled. "And now," he says to his heart, "be at rest forever; thou hast palpitated long enough. Nothing here is worthy of thy throbbings; this world deserves no sigh." It is the language of utter failure, disappointment, despair.

But perhaps (2) the future of humanity on earth may offer something better. There is a present joy in toiling for a future good. The noble heart bears its own pain and grief willingly when it thinks of the glorious future which it is helping to work out for the race to which it belongs. But even this, he says, is an illusion. If man's existence was ever tolerable, it was when he was as the beast that perishes. What we call progress is only increase of misery. He that increaseth what is called knowledge only increaseth sorrow. Culture has only added to our wretchedness by making us acquainted with the hopelessness of our condition. The best thing that could have happened would have been that we should not exist at all; the next best thing is that we should cease to exist.

But (3) there is a third way. There may be

happiness in a future world, and men may bear much here for the sake of the eternal glory into which they shall enter hereafter. To this the Pessimist can only reply that there is no hereafter. Yet he is not quite sure of this. But at least he recognizes no duty to the future. Self-destruction he holds to be perfectly lawful. Once or twice he was on the point of committing suicide, but his regard for others prevented him from inflicting additional suffering upon them. Besides, he was otherwise inconsistent in shrinking at the prospect of death. He fled to escape the approach of cholera; so that existence did not then appear to him as an unmitigated evil.

The moral of this terrible system is not far to seek, and we shall have presently to indicate it more distinctly. We must now, however, pass from Leopardi to a name much better known and of far wider and deeper influence,—that of the German, Arthur Schopenhauer.

As far as regards their general view of human life, the system of Schopenhauer and of his greatest disciple and successor, Hartmann, is substantially the same as that of Leopardi. In their view also, existence is an evil; life is not worth living; those who assist in propagating the species are the greatest enemies of their kind. The best thing that could be done for it, the most merciful, the kindest thing, would be to extinguish the whole race, not by a universal suicide, which would seem to be the speediest mode of escape, but by a voluntary asceticism, deliberately chosen from the settled conviction that there is nothing in the world that a man ought to care for, and therefore the highest wisdom is pure indifference and absolute insensibility. It is, as we have said, Buddhism over again. The highest perfection is *Nirvâna,* — the destruction of thought, desire, feeling, conscious being.

In this respect the Italian poet and the German philosophers are in complete agreement. The difference between them lies in this, that Leopardi's opinions were the outcome of his own temperament and circumstances, and his illustration of them was drawn chiefly from the obvious facts of experience, while Schopenhauer and Hartmann have endeavored to elaborate a philosophical system. With these systems we shall here deal no further than our subject demands. Most of us probably will be willing to confess that we do not understand them and never shall. But there is no special difficulty in making out their theory of pessimism.

It has already been remarked that the great Leibnitz was an optimist, perhaps an extreme optimist; and optimism was the prevailing theory in Germany during the last century and at the beginning of the present. Before the time of Schopenhauer there had, it is true, been some scattered utterances showing some traces of a darker tendency. Fichte, for example, had said that the actual world was the worst of all possible worlds; but this did not represent, as in the case of Schopenhauer, his deliberate judgment. Schelling had declared that sorrow and suffering were necessary elements in human life; and expressions of a similar character may be found in Kant and his successors.

But the kind of pessimism, if it may be so called, which was countenanced by these writers, had very little affinity with the systems we are now considering, and hardly went further than many Christians are inclined to go. There are many believers in the Gospel of Jesus Christ who regard this world as a mere vale of tears, full of sorrow and suffering and weeping and lamentation. There are many who think it is going from bad to worse day after day, and that all prospect of improving is so much worse than uncertain that any effort in that direction is wasted labor. But such persons, be they right or wrong, are not pessimists in the present sense of the word. They believe that there is a better life in a perfect world beyond the present; they believe that all things are working together for good, and that, whatever the end may be, it will result in the promotion of the glory of God, in the manifestation of His infinite and eternal perfections. Such a belief, whatever form it may take, is obviously a species of optimism.

The pessimism of Schopenhauer is absolute

and deadly, and it is carefully reasoned. According to him, all suffering and all evil is from the *Will*. By the will he means something widely different from that self-determining faculty in man which is generally recognized as the basis of his responsibility. He means almost exactly what scientific men mean by the word *Force;* for, according to him, the principle of *will* is a blind and unconscious desire of life, — a desire which arises in some inexplicable manner, and determines the character of all kinds of being, through all the various stages of existence.

This blind force, or will, develops itself first in inorganic Nature, then in the vegetable world, next in the animal world, and finally it arrives at consciousness in man. And thus it becomes the principle of suffering and misery. Evil had existed before, but it was felt rather than known. It is in man that a full consciousness of suffering is realized. To him, above all other creatures, life involves effort, and effort is suffering. He cannot help putting forth these efforts; necessity constrains him to do it. But the need is not perfectly satisfied; and even when it seems to be so, the satisfaction is an illusion, and leads to new needs and new sorrows. "The life of man," as he puts it, " is but a struggle for existence, with the certainty of being vanquished." Hence he draws these two conclusions: (1) That all pleasure is negative, and suffering alone is positive; (2) That the more human intelligence increases, the more is man sensible to suffering; in other words, that what is called progress is but the sure means of increasing human misery.

From all this there can be but one inference; namely, that it is the duty of every man, if any such thing as duty can any longer be assumed, to devise means for the extinction of that existence whose only positive possession is suffering, and whose advancement in all that constitutes what we call culture and civilization can mean only an increase of hopeless wretchedness.

What are we to think of this system? Whence does it come? To what will it lead? How are we to deal with it? These are questions which we cannot afford to neglect. Pessimism has, up to the present time, obtained no solid footing in England or America; but it has become a raging epidemic in Germany, and from thence it is spreading to France and Italy, and indeed there are not wanting signs that it has infected many among ourselves.

II. What are we to think of pessimism as regards the truth of its main principles? Is it true that effort produces misery only, or chiefly? Is it true that our misery is something positive, while our pleasure is merely negative? Does the progress of the species mean essentially the increase of misery? These are primary questions.

1. In the first place, we admit that life involves the putting forth of force, energy, will; and that life like ours involves conscious effort. This is perfectly clear. But is it so clear that effort brings in its train nothing but suffering, or that the pleasure which accompanies it is merely negative? This is a question which appeals to human experience, and which can be answered in no other way. We have no hesitation in affirming that the testimony of experience is precisely the reverse of what the pessimist affirms. Experience tells us that effort is a pleasure, a joy.

Make what deductions you please, in the obstacles which we encounter while we seek to reach our ends, in the difficulty of triumphing over those obstacles, in the fatigue which results from the efforts which are made; these deductions will never serve to neutralize the pleasure of effort, the joy of the struggle, to the worker, the combatant, the athlete. Nay, in those very difficulties he finds a new source of joy and delight. At the presence of obstacles his spirit is stirred and braced for the encounter; in the most strenuous endeavors to succeed there may indeed be pain, but there mingles with it the keenest pleasure; and as regards the fatigue resulting from effort, who is there that has really known the sweetness of rest and repose without having first experienced the pain of toil and the sense of weariness and fatigue?

Nor do these elements of pleasure complete the circle. The laborer is urged on by the prospect of success. The joy which is set before him enables him to make light of the pain which he endures; and he is even more nobly sustained by the sense of duty, which adds the approval of conscience as the best and highest element in the satisfaction which he experiences.

This is not a question which can be settled by speculation; it is a simple question of experience, and we may appeal not only to the literature of all ages, but to the life of all ages. Effort is not always produced by sheer necessity; it is itself an instinctive product of life; it is put forth out of an inward necessity, and it is the source of true enjoyment to man. Here we are touching the very foundation of the subject. If the system is wrong here, it is radically wrong, and no correctness in details can justify it as a system. Let us, however, pass on to the subordinate principles of the theory.

2. According to Schopenhauer, pleasure, where it exists, is only negative; pain alone is positive. A state of pain is, in fact, man's normal condition; and pleasure is but the momentary cessation of pain, the suspension of the suffering which is the habitual attendant of existence. Effort, suffering, death, — this is the positive history of mankind.

It ought to be noticed that Hartmann here dissents from his master. He points out, in fact, that Schopenhauer makes as great a mistake on the one side as Leibnitz had done on the other. According to Leibnitz, pain was a mere negation of pleasure, which alone was positive. This was an evident paradox. If human consciousness is worth anything, — if it be worth nothing, it is of no use discussing these or any other questions of the same kind, — if human consciousness is worth anything, then pain is often something very positive, and not a mere negation of pleasure.

But, on the other hand, Schopenhauer equally contradicted conscious experience when he refused a positive character to pleasure. There are undoubtedly pleasures which are, in a sense, negative. There are pleasures of which we may be said to be habitually unconscious, of the existence of which we are made aware only when we are subjected to pain more or less acute. It is when that pain obtains alleviation that the negative pleasure becomes for a moment, as it were, positive, and we are made fully conscious of the privilege which in that respect we enjoyed. But it is equally certain that there are pleasures which are obviously and undoubtedly positive, which are not mere intervals between attacks of pain, — pleasures which may vanish without any consciousness of evil or pain coming in their place. If these are not positive, we confess we do not know the meaning of the word. The determination of this question, when it is once clearly stated, may safely be left to the common sense of mankind.

3. One other point of detail remains, — namely, the assertion that life is a misery and an evil in proportion to its development and elevation. This notion is a natural inference from the theory that life in itself is an evil. If so, then, of course, the more abundant the life, the greater the evil of existence. Pain begins with sensation, — it may be difficult to say where, because it is difficult to detect the first traces of sensation; but there is no doubt that, as organization becomes more perfect and more refined, the organized being becomes more intensely conscious of pain, more keenly alive to every cause by which pain may be produced.

Here at least, then, the pessimist is, superficially at least, in the right. Man suffers far more acutely than the mere animal. Shakespeare, if we may venture thus to speak of one so great, was clearly mistaken when he said that the harmless beetle that we tread upon feels a pang as great as when a giant dies. And it is not merely that man's sensations are far keener than those of the mere animal: he has sources of suffering to which the brute creation are strangers. He feels at the moment more keenly than the animal; but, as has been well said, "he eternizes pain by memory, he anticipates it by his foresight, he multiplies it incalculably by his imagination: he does not, like the animal, suffer only in the present; he torments himself by the past and future, to say nothing of that vast contingent of moral pains of which the animal has no experience."[1]

To this extent, of course, the pessimist is right. Man does suffer in many ways that do not touch the mere animal. And if pessimism had gone no further, we should here have had no controversy with it. The differences even between man and man, in respect of sensibility, are astonishing. In the lower types of humanity men will bear injuries to the body which would positively madden those who belong to the higher types. It is clear, then, that there is the closest connection between man's sensitiveness to pain and his intellectual development.

Must we then, in asserting these facts, admit the inferences which are deduced from them by pessimists? Are we bound to say, that, because increased intelligence is associated with a finer organization and therefore with increased liability to suffering, therefore intelligence is an

---

[1] This thought is finely expressed by Burns in his "Address to a Mouse:" —

> " Still thou art blest compared wi' me !
> The present only toucheth thee :
> But, oh ! I backward cast my e'e
>   On prospects drear !
> An' forward, tho' I canna see
>   I guess an' fear ! "

evil and nothing else; that the lower a man is in the scale of civilization, the happier, or rather the less miserable, he is; that the ordinary commonplace man is happier than the man of genius, the animal than the man, the lowest type of animal than the highest, — in short, that the state of insensibility and unconsciousness is the best of all? As Hartmann puts it, "Let us think of the happiness in which we see an ox or pig living, or of the happiness of the proverbial fish in the water! Still more enviable than the life of the fish must be that of the oyster, and better still the life of the plant. We go down, in fact, below consciousness, and individual suffering disappears with it."

Such is the logical conclusion of pessimism as expressed by Hartmann; but it is also the *Reductio ad absurdum* of the system. There is, in fact, no difficulty in furnishing an answer to it when it is presented to us in this form. It is the answer that springs instinctively to every man's lips, which bids him protest that it is better to be a man than a brute. It is, indeed, difficult for us to estimate the relative value of different kinds of pleasure; yet we know that the higher pleasures have a value altogether incommensurable with the lower. We do not place them side by side for the sake of comparison, for there is no possibility of comparison between them.

"I suppose," says M. Caro, "that Newton,

when he found the exact formula of the law of attraction, condensed into a single moment more of joy than all the gourmands of London can taste in the course of a whole year in their taverns, with their venison pasties and their pots of ale. Pascal was a sufferer throughout the whole of the thirty-nine years during which his life lasted. Can it be imagined that the clear view which he first obtained of the two infinites, which no one until then had grasped so firmly, in their mysterious analogy and in their contrast, — can it be imagined that such a view did not fill this great mind with a happiness proportioned to its greatness, with a joy whose intoxication surpassed all vulgar joys, and which for a moment suspended all his sufferings? Who would not rather be Shakespeare than Falstaff? Who would not rather be Molière than the *Bourgeois Gentilhomme*, — that combination of wealth and stupidity?"

Nor does instinct deceive us in this preference. Reason is unhesitatingly on the same side. It tells us, with a force which leaves no doubt in our minds, that it is better to be a man than to be a hog, because man thinks; and thought, which is the source of much suffering, is also the source of purer and higher joys than any which are derived from sense. The supreme misery is not to be a man, but, being a man, so to despise one's nature as to regret that one is not a mere animal. It is possible that such regrets may exist. There are many whose only ideas of happiness are connected with the gratification of the senses, who are never satisfied except when indulging those appetites which they possess in common with the brutes. It is natural that such men should think the life of the mere animal the best. It is natural that they should despise that higher nature of intelligence and moral consciousness which, even in the most degraded, will sometimes interrupt what they call their enjoyments. But they will find it difficult to convince the mass of their fellow-men that they are right. Even those who are not keenly alive to the highest exercises of the intellect, the heart, the spirit which is akin to the Divinity, will hesitate to sacrifice the purer joys of friendship, affection, social intercourse, for the sake of wallowing in the sty of the sensualist. When this inevitable result of pessimism is once clearly understood, humanity will rise against it. The old assertion of innate human dignity will be put forth: "Homo sum" (I am a man); and man is higher and better than the brute that perishes.

To this protest of man's instincts, reason, conscience, what has pessimism to reply? It can only say that men deceive themselves; that this notion of their superiority and of the happiness resulting from it is a mere illusion. You are not the happier, you are not the better, for these imagined transports of the intellect, the imagination, the heart; it is a mere self-deception. You are the slave of some blind force which is leading you onward, only to leave you at last, freed from your delusions, sunk in a deeper misery.

There is, in fact, no other escape for pessimism. And yet what is this but a pure begging of the question? To conduct an argument proving the utter misery of mankind, and then to deny the testimony of human consciousness, is not to prove that the life of man upon earth is a life of wretchedness, but only that it ought to be. And here the system falls to the ground; its proofs are utterly inadequate to support its conclusions. For the question is not as to the existence of pain, sorrow, and suffering on earth, nor even as to the proportion which these bear in the life of man, collective or individual, — for these are questions not easily solved. The question is as to the utter badness, misery, and hopelessness of man's life as it is; and we repeat that this is not in any way proved. Men still believe that existence is better than annihilation, that the existence of man is better than that of the brute.

If the pessimist persists in disbelieving this, we ask for the source of his convictions and he gives us only human experience; and there can be no other court of appeal. A man can be called unhappy only because he feels himself to be so. A man cannot be said to be in pain unless he is conscious of it. The foundation, therefore, of the pessimist argument is laid in that very consciousness which he rejects when it is against him. How easy it is to turn the rejection of this testimony against the pessimist himself! You say that man is miserable; but we do not believe it. We say, on the contrary, that man is happy. Granting that there is much of suffering and of pain, we yet find so much to counterbalance all this, that we are inclined to say, with Paley, " It is a happy world, after all!"

But we may go further: we also may deny the testimony of consciousness to human misery. You say you are unhappy, but we do not believe it. It is a mere illusion of your imagination. These sorrows of yours are unreal; these sufferings are imaginary, the creation of a bewildered fancy. Who shall say that this retort is invalid? It is at least as good as the denial of the testimony of consciousness to human worth and dignity. Nay, it is better; for there are few who can look back upon their past experience, and say that there was no good reason for their happiness and their joy; but there are multitudes who can recall troubles of their own making, fears which had their origin simply in a morbid state of mind, presentiments of whose origin no reasonable account could be given, and which had no fulfilment in the future.

We return, therefore, to our assertion that man's consciousness must be accepted as a credible witness, and that we possess, as an indestructible fact of consciousness, the conviction that our life on earth is great, good, and blessed, not in proportion as life fades and loses its energy and sinks into unconsciousness and annihilation, but, on the contrary, as it rises in energy and power, as it becomes freer from the influences from beneath and more open to those which are from above, as it becomes less animal and more spiritual, as it partakes less of earth and more of heaven, as it grows less and less like the life of the brute and more and more like the life of God.

But there is another consideration which ought not to be passed over. Whatever man's earthly life may be, it is not final. We believe that we are here in a state of discipline for a better life beyond. This is not the end; it is but the way. This is not the goal; it is but the course. To judge of man's whole life, to estimate the whole worth and importance of his existence by the part which is now before us, is like judging of a man's whole history on earth by his days at school. If there be a future for man, if there be a life of manhood beyond the present, for which the present is only a childhood of preparation, then no estimate of man's life can pretend to completeness which does not take account of that future existence.

III. It is a matter of the greatest interest to account for the origin and sources of this movement; and various attempts have been made to explain its existence and its diffusion and influence, especially in Germany.

Looking at the individual aspect of the subject, we see clearly that pessimism is often the result of temperament and constitution. Some men are naturally cheerful, and others naturally gloomy. Some anticipate evils; others never care to think of them until they are called upon to face them. Some are easily satisfied; others are morbidly discontented. We can in this way explain exceptional and individual cases of pessimism; but such solutions do not touch the question in its wider aspects.

Some have attempted to explain the malady, as it is truly called, by the manner of life prevalent among the people whom it has most deeply infected. According to their explanation, the reasons of pessimism are chiefly chemical. People who drink beer and other heavy liquors, they say, are generally pessimists; those who drink light wines are optimists. This is the reason, says an illustrious French chemist, why pessimism has its home in Germany. "There is no fear," he says, "of its ever becoming acclimatized in the lands of the vine, nor, above all, in France; the wine of Bordeaux clears men's ideas, and the wine of Burgundy puts the nightmare to flight."

Such an explanation, like the other, may contain a measure of truth. But its scope is too limited: it does not explain the facts with which we have now to deal; it does not set aside the difficulty by which we are now confronted. There have always been these differences of men and manners. Germans have drunk beer and Frenchmen have drunk light wines for centuries; but this does not tell us why in this present century the disease of pessimism has broken out in Germany, and has spread among the thinkers of that land, and is now invading every civilized country, so that its influence may be extensively traced in the contemporaneous literature of every European people and in America. We have mentioned England, France, and Italy. It is said that it has also spread far and wide in Russia: its presence is seen in Nihilism; and it has appeared among the Slavonian races in general.

For this new and striking phenomenon we must seek out a specific cause; and it is to be found partly in the history of the German nation, and partly in the state of religious belief.

With respect to the former of these two causes, that which is found in the history of the German people, the subject is evidently too great and too intricate to be disentangled here, even if we were qualified to undertake such a work. The history of Germany from the close of the Thirty Years' War, when that great people were left little better than a mutilated and dying body, is one of the most remarkable that the world has ever seen; and the process by which it has recovered life, strength, energy, is full of instruction. By its own internal vitality, by the wisdom of its rulers, and the ability of its military chiefs, it has risen from a condition in which it was tolerated, and alternately patronized and chastised by its powerful neighbors, to a condition in which it can do more than hold its own; and in this history the thoughtful student will find something to explain the strange course taken by German thought.

If, again, the religions and philosophies and philosophical tendencies and theories, which have alternately emerged into prominence and sunk into neglect, are considered, — the outbursts of faith on the one side, and of unbelief on the other, — the alternation of dogmatism, religious and philosophical, with scepticism, — we shall hardly wonder that men grew bewildered, dizzy, and hardly knew whether they stood on earth or on air.

But one thing at least comes out clearly, and it is this, — that the system of pessimism could rise and flourish only on the ruins of Christian belief. Let life be never so unsatisfying, the man who believes that there is an ideal life, after which he may strive and which he may hope to attain, will not be altogether intolerant or impatient of the real. The present truly has its pains, its sorrows, its disappointments. But he who believes in a future in which all evil shall be put away, all wrongs righted, all misdoings redressed, will find it easier to regard the present, if not with perfect complacency, at least with patience. If the end of the journey is rest, peace, and joy, the roughest of the road will be trodden, if sometimes with pain, yet also with cheerfulness, by him who believes that, while the pain is momentary, the joy is everlasting.

The other side of the alternative is equally plain. The man who has lost all faith in God and all hope of immortality, if he really thinks and feels, will almost inevitably come to regard life and existence as a very questionable good, if not an unmixed evil. And here, we fully concede, there is a certain measure of truth in the pessimist's view of comparative happiness. No doubt there are men who live a mere animal life, destitute of the finer feelings of our nature, little sensitive even to physical pain, utterly ignorant of any other form of suffering, who have a low kind of enjoyment which leaves no place for reflection. To them life is no evil, and the loss of life nothing to shrink from, because they live — if indeed we can say that they live — in the present, and enjoy those lower pleasures of which they are capable. Yet even these may have their waking moments, or dreams of terror to break their sleep.

If, on the other hand, we take, not the highest examples of noble human cultivation, but the average man or woman who lives in the midst of our social system, we cannot wonder that those among us who have lost their faith in God and an unseen world should look upon the life which they have as worthless and miserable. What earthly possession of man is sure? What source of human happiness is there that may not in a moment be dried up?

You are rich, and your wealth ministers to refinement and every earthly good for yourself, and it is generously expended for the good of others; but Fate waves her cruel rod and your riches take to themselves wings. You are strong and healthy, and glory in the rich abundance of energy and vigor with which you are endowed; but sickness casts its baleful eye upon you, and you wither and decay. You have friends who are dear to you as life, and you find in their fellowship joys as intense and ravishing as they are pure and elevating; but the angel of death strikes at the best and dearest, and your life is bruised by the blow which has shattered another. No rank, no power, no goodness or graciousness, will protect the old or the young in the dread encounter.

If there be a God and a life to come, we can bear these things. We can smile through our tears as we see the guiding Hand which leads us through the wilderness. Faith assures us that all is well done, because it is done by One who is wiser and more loving than we, and who will never lay upon us more than He will give us strength to endure. If we believe in God, and hope for His glory, then we cannot be pessimists, we cannot believe that all is for the worst; we cannot help believing that all is for the best, that all things work together for good, and that our light affliction, which is for a moment, is working for us more and more exceedingly an eternal weight of glory.

But if none of these things be so, if there be no God and no hereafter, then we cannot wonder that men grow desperate about life. If all is fate or chance, if our poor existence is tossed about by blind unconscious forces, of which we know not whence they come or whither they go, then indeed life is an evil and a misery, a distraction from which we may well seek to escape. If we could raise our eyes to the blue vault of heaven, and believe that those celestial orbs that roll above us are guided by no Divine will; if we could look down upon this green earth, and think that it was the grave of our kind, and that no blessed vernal season could come and bring back from their winter sleep the bright and beautiful flowers that had sunk into the bosom of Nature,—then we should take the pessimist by the hand, and welcome him as a brother, as a friend and benefactor of his race. You are right, we would say to him. These joys and hopes are vain illusions, for they rest upon the baseless dream of immortality; let us tread them under foot. These flowers of love and duty are but weeds on this existence-cursed earth; let us tear them up and cast them into the fire. This education and self-discipline at which we are laboring with unceasing toil is but a ladder upon which men are climbing higher and higher into the clouds and tempests which overshadow and trouble their life. Down with it, down with it, even to the ground! Down with knowledge and wisdom, with virtue and goodness, with love and truth! Down with thought and feeling and consciousness and existence; for they are evils and miseries! Down with the life of man; for the life of the brutes is better! "Let us eat and drink, for to-morrow we die." Let us extinguish and annihilate the race of man, for existence itself is an evil. This is the pessimist gospel; and if there be no God, then there can be no other good news for the children of men.

It is sometimes urged against the revelation of God in Jesus Christ, that it leaves many difficulties in the life of man unravelled, many knots untied. We freely admit it; and remembering what human life is, we should be surprised if it were otherwise. But this we can say fearlessly and confidently, that there is no single fact in the history of mankind which is not made easier of understanding by the light of the Gospel. We at least know who and what our God is, what He means by this order of things in which we live, what He has done for us, what He is doing for us; and we also know — we certainly believe, and we think that we know — that He will bring order out of confusion, and good out of evil. And who, besides the Christian, has any clear notion of the meaning and the issues of human life? What can the deist say? To him the Creator is but an unknown God, and he can only guess as to His purposes in fear and perplexity. He may hope and believe that all will come right in the end, but he knows nothing of the manner in which it is being accomplished. And what can the atheist say? He can say nothing. He cannot even assure you that there is not a God. At the very utmost he is but an agnostic. He knows nothing, and he can tell nothing, of any sphere which is beyond the realm of sense.

Tell him that you are tortured by doubts and fears, and he can only reply that he can neither remove the one nor alleviate the other. Tell him that you want to know something about the future, and he will reply that he cannot help you; he cannot even assure you that there will be no future. Tell him that you find this life poor and aimless and worthless, unless it is the way to a better, and he must answer that he knows of nothing better, of nothing besides; and you must make the best or the worst of this life as you like and as you can.

And this is the last word of positivism. It ends in this dismal pessimism, whose philosophy is despair, and whose solace is annihilation. Go forth with this gospel to the toiling, suffering children of men, and what will it do for them? Will it make them braver, happier, better men? No! it will only tell them that happiness is a delusion, and goodness an empty name.

It is in presence of theories like these that we feel more deeply than ever that, through whatever trials the Church of Christ may pass, we have no fear for the Gospel of our salvation. We have no fear for it, because we know that men, driven by the cravings of their hearts, will still seek for the living God, will rejoice to hear of the Word " made flesh," of the Godhead enshrined in truest, gentlest, most loving manhood, upon whose bosom the weary head may lay itself down in perfect trust and find unbroken repose, from whose cheering voice the wearied heart will receive a new stimulus for the battle of life.

We have no fear for it, because it is true, — true to the instincts of the human heart, true as meeting the demands of the severest criticism, true as vindicating for itself an unquestionable place in the history of the world as a revelation from God.

LECTURE VII.

THE RESURRECTION OF JESUS CHRIST.

PART I.

EXAMINATION OF THE EVIDENCE FOR THE RESURRECTION.

1. Introductory. — Importance of the Event. — The Gospel founded on Facts. — Necessity of Revelation for the Support of Religious Truth. — 2. The Fact of the Resurrection. — Its Meaning. — 3. The Nature of the Evidence. — No Evidence sufficient for those who disbelieve in the Supernatural. — The Existence of a Personal God postulated. — The Church exists and professes to have the Knowledge of God by Revelation. — The Burden of Proof not entirely with the Christian. — Points on which there is general Agreement. — The Documentary Proof. — Two Questions: (1) What did the Disciples of Christ believe? (2) Are we justified in believing the Same? — 4. The Evidence of the Gospel Histories; their Agreement; their Statements. — Objections: Not seen to rise; Disagreement as to the Time, as to the Circumstances; Legendary Details. — Answers. — Final Verdict on Evidence. — 5. The Evidence of Saint Paul. — Documents admitted. — Points of Agreement. — What the admitted Documents assert. — An independent Testimony. — Its Value affected by the Character of the Witness. — Objections to his Testimony. — Answers. — The Value of Saint Paul's Testimony. — Disingenuous and inconsistent Objection. — Answer.

1. INTRODUCTORY.

IT is unnecessary to dwell at any length upon the supreme importance of a belief in the resurrection of Jesus Christ from the dead.

This is, indeed, one of those great facts which form an essential part of the Gospel history and testimony. An unbeliever could see that it was represented by Saint Paul " as above all, the culminating point of Christian doctrine."[1] It is at once the top stone of the fabric of divine revelation, and the greatest of the miraculous evidences for the supernatural character of the work of Christ.

The importance of this event has been clearly perceived by both sides in the Christian controversy, by believers and unbelievers alike; and accordingly every effort has been made by the adversaries of the Gospel to destroy the grounds of our belief, while the defenders of the Christian faith have made their confident appeal to reason and to history in support of the truth of their Lord's rising again.

"If the Resurrection really took place," says a recent assailant[2] of its reality, "then Christianity may [rather, *must*] be admitted to be what it claims to be, a direct revelation from God. Nay, the Resurrection is not merely a voucher for revelation, it may truly be said to be in itself a revelation." "If Christ be not risen," says Saint Paul, "then is our preaching vain, and your faith is also vain." Both sides are equally clear as to the result of a failure to

---

[1] Baur, quoted by Macan in his Hibbert Essay on "The Resurrection of Jesus Christ," p. 4.

[2] Macan, The Resurrection of Jesus Christ, p. 6.

make good their own contention. The unbeliever freely admits that he must neutralize the proof adduced in support of the alleged fact or become a believer. The Christian Apostle tells us as plainly that, if the Resurrection cannot be believed, then there is nothing left to believe.

In this respect there is really no difference between our own position and that of believers in the first age of the Church. The destruction of this foundation would be as dangerous to a rational faith now as ever it was. It has indeed been maintained, that, while a belief in the Resurrection was necessary in order to the very existence of the Christian Church, it may be now dispensed with, and yet our faith will remain unaffected. The first of these allegations may be accepted without hesitation, while the second is most certainly false.

But for a belief in the resurrection of Jesus, the Church would never have existed. This is too obvious to be seriously called in question. Even Strauss declares that the historical importance of the Resurrection is such that, "without a belief in it, a Christian community would hardly have come together."[1] "But," it has been urged,[2] "now that it has come together, and existed for centuries, it might dispense with that belief without forfeiting its existence. The life and death of Christ, His person and His

---

[1] Strauss, Leben Jesu für das deutsche Volk, § 97.
[2] Macan, p. 6.

teaching, — these are what are of permanent and essential importance to men, and not a supposed event miraculously performed on Him, and which is neither in itself essential to His 'method and secret,' nor represented as essentially connected with them in the New Testament."

There are several statements here which we should be unable to accept; but the main point on which we differ from the writer is that which is concerned with the comparative necessity or usefulness of a belief in the resurrection of Christ in the days of the Apostles and in our own times. As a mere argument for the truth of the Gospel story, the belief of the Resurrection is not less necessary, but more necessary, now than it was then. The truth of this assertion we must endeavor to make good.

Let it be remembered, first of all, that, according to the representations of the New Testament, the facts of the Gospel are the sources of its power and the very foundation of its doctrines. One instance may suffice. When Saint Paul was making known to the Corinthians, in a formal manner, the Gospel which he preached to them, that Gospel which they had received and wherein they stood, he said: " I delivered unto you first of all that which also I received, how that Christ died for our sins according to the scriptures; and that he was buried, and that He hath been raised on the third day according to the scriptures," and so forth.[1] Now, the Apostle clearly puts forth the enunciation of these *facts* as the preaching of the Gospel; and prominent among them — for it is that fact of which he proceeds to offer copious proof — he places the resurrection of Christ.

Nor is it difficult to understand the importance of historical facts as the vehicle of a Divine Revelation. Consider only, without going further, the elementary truths of human responsibility, the existence and the character of Almighty God, and you will see that we have gained our clearest notions of these truths from the life and words and works and death and resurrection of our Lord Jesus Christ. It is a simple truth of history that "the world by wisdom knew not God." The statement of our Lord that the Father is revealed by the only-begotten Son is verified in the experience of the Christian and the Church. Take away this revelation, and are you sure that you can keep alive a belief in those principles of religion and morality which are connected with it?

Even if we were satisfied of the sufficiency of what are called the permanent principles of religion which are retained by those who reject the supernatural element in religion (although how there can be a religion without a supernatural element it might puzzle us to determine), are we quite sure that these beliefs can be main-

[1] 1 Cor. xv. 3, 4.

tained without the support of revelation? As a matter of fact, they are denied by most of those who reject revelation; and the great mass of mankind could retain no hold upon them without this support. It is not enough to tell men that certain truths are self-evident, or that they may be demonstrated by sufficient arguments; they must be satisfied that they have the authority of God. When we can commend a truth to the human conscience by the unfaltering declaration, "Thus saith the Lord," then we have put forth a claim to attention which is unique, and, if well grounded, irresistible.

Now, if there be any force in these considerations, it is clear that the truth of the Resurrection is of far greater importance to us than to the first disciples of Jesus Christ, for this simple reason, — that it is to us the most powerful assurance of the truth of His teaching and work. In the days of Saint Paul there were many persons alive who had seen the Lord Jesus in life, who had listened to His teaching, who had been witnesses of His miraculous power, some at least who had been the subjects of His gracious power to bless. To such persons there was no doubt of His Messiahship, none of His truth, His wisdom, His power, or His love. Even if we could suppose them uncertain or ignorant of the fact of His resurrection, they still would have no doubt of His general character and work. With ourselves the case is quite different.

To us the Resurrection is not only the greatest of all the miracles connected with His manifestation, but the surest. In a certain sense it is the support and guarantee of all the other miracles. If we doubt, or abandon belief in, the truth of the Resurrection, we shall hardly retain faith in any of the signs shown by our Lord, or even in the mere principle of the supernatural. Let this, then, be clearly understood as our position. If we are forced to give up the Resurrection, we must give up Christianity as a revelation from God. If the Resurrection can be conclusively maintained, then Christ was a Saviour sent from God.

2. THE FACT OF THE RESURRECTION.

Before we inquire into the nature of the evidence, we must ask what we mean by the fact which we assert, the Resurrection of Jesus Christ from the dead. The faith of the Church is thus stated in our fourth Article: "Christ did truly rise again from death, and took again His body, with flesh, bones, and all things appertaining to the perfection of man's nature." It has been truly said by one of the assailants[1] of the doctrine: "We have nothing to do here with the vague modern representation of these events, by means of which the objective facts vanish,

---

[1] Supernatural Religion (complete English edition in three volumes), vol. iii. p. 400. Compare Macan, p. 27.

and are replaced by subjective impressions and tricks of consciousness, or symbols of spiritual life. Those who adopt such views have, of course, abandoned all that is real and supernatural in the supposed events. The Resurrection and Ascension which we have to deal with are events precisely as objective and real as the death and burial, — no ideal process figured by the imagination or embodiments of Christian hope, but tangible realities, historical occurrences in the sense of ordinary life. If Jesus, after being crucified, dead, and buried, did not physically [the word is ambiguous, but we let it pass] rise again from the dead, and in the flesh [again ambiguous], without again dying, 'ascend into heaven,' the whole case falls to the ground."

We accept, generally, this statement of the question; and it is the more important to insist upon the objective reality of the occurrence, that writers and even preachers,[1] who profess to be Christians, continue to use language respecting the great facts of our Lord's resurrection and ascension which would seem to imply that they have no more than an ideal value, or at least that this is the only aspect of the matter which it is important to preserve. Such a notion is a pure delusion, and a subversion of what

---

[1] As an example, we may mention one of the most eloquent of German preachers, Dr. Schwartz, the Court Chaplain at Gotha.

we mean by the faith of the Church and the reality of the Christian Revelation. If Christ be not actually and objectively risen, then our faith is vain. We cannot retain the ideas, if we abandon the facts. The Resurrection which we maintain is a real one. We entirely agree with the writer just quoted, that "these incidents, although stupendous miracles, must also have been actual occurrences." If they did not really take place, our task is at an end. If it is asserted that they really did take place, their occurrence must be attested by adequate evidence.[1] We acknowledge the reasonableness of this demand. We believe that these occurrences actually took place, and that they are proved by sufficient evidence.

3. THE NATURE OF THE EVIDENCE.

Of what nature must the evidence be that will satisfy us of the truth of the Resurrection? This is our next question. And what is the common ground that we may assume as a starting-point, conceded alike by our opponents and ourselves?

One thing is quite clear, that no evidences will suffice for those who take it for granted that all miracles are impossible, or at least so improbable as to be incredible. And yet this is the starting-point of many who assail the truth of this and all the other miracles of the Gospel.

[1] Supernatural Religion, vol. iii. p. 401.

They start with a perfect certainty that no amount of evidence can give assurance of the truth of the facts which they profess to investigate, and then they bend all their energies to prove that the evidences adduced are insufficient.

The difference between ourselves and our adversaries is indeed fundamental. We believe in a personal God, and, for the most part, they do not. Certainly, if there is a God who takes an interest in His creatures, it cannot be thought surprising that He should adopt some method of making His will more perfectly known to them. If our argument were merely with deists, such a suggestion might be a sufficient introduction to a consideration of the evidence. Most of our opponents will not, however, allow us this starting-point. We must, therefore, meet them in another way. At least we can say it is not certain that there is no God. There may be a God, and He may have made some supernatural revelation of Himself to His creatures. At any rate, there has been for ages in existence a society, the Christian Church, which professes to have such a revelation, and to have satisfactory evidence of its having come from God. Is it too much to ask that men shall give a careful and candid consideration to these evidences? We do not ask the inquirer to be satisfied with trifling proofs; we do not ask him to accept sentiments for arguments, or hopes for realities. We simply ask that he shall be willing to look fairly at the evidences which are adduced in support of an alleged fact of the greatest moment in regard to human belief.

Let us consider how the subject presents itself to us in the history of mankind. On the most superficial view of the matter we see before us a long and deeply interesting history, the history of Christianity and of the Church, which, by the admission of all, has sprung out of a *belief* in the resurrection of Jesus Christ from the dead. We discern in this Body, which is called the Church of Christ, and in this system of teaching, which is called the Gospel of Christ, a mighty moral power which has penetrated, leavened, moulded the whole of human society in the most civilized nations of the world for many centuries. And we ask, Has this history, has this power, taken its beginning from a falsehood or a delusion?

Surely, in such a case the whole burden of proof is not with ourselves! Even if we were unable to give a complete account of this vast system in which we find ourselves, men might yet hesitate to assail it and destroy it as an imposture. In such a case we may say with confidence, apart from all minute historical investigations into the origin of the Church, the probability is not entirely on the side of unbelief. We are not using this argument as a reason for being satisfied with insufficient evidences on behalf of the facts of Christianity; but we do urge that such considerations may give some confidence to the Christian apologist in his work, and induce the doubter and the unbeliever to come to the inquiry with some amount of sympathy, or at least with a sentiment of strict impartiality.

So much may be said for what may be called the principles of our inquiry. We must now approach the facts, — first, those which are generally, if not universally, admitted, and afterwards those which we are required to prove.

It is agreed on all hands that Jesus Christ was the Founder of the Christian religion and Church, and that He lived in the age of the world to which His life and work are assigned by the Christian creeds. It is agreed that the Christian Church arose at a period close to the time of his death, in the reign of Tiberius Cæsar, the Roman Emperor. It is agreed that a belief in the resurrection of Jesus Christ from the dead lay at the foundation of the Church and its faith.[1] When we further ask what are the grounds of that belief, — why, in short, the resurrection of Christ should be accepted as an objective fact rather than as a legend or a myth, like the beliefs of many other religions, — we are directed to a series of documents which profess to be written by men who had themselves seen

[1] This is fully conceded by Strauss and his followers, and by the Tübingen School generally.

our Lord, or had received their information from those who had been His companions.

Thus we have four sets of memoirs of the life and teaching of Jesus on earth, — two of them professing to be written by His own companions and Apostles, one by a writer who is said to have been the companion of Saint Peter, and another by a writer who was the companion of Saint Paul, and who says that he obtained his information from those who had perfect knowledge of the matters which he records.

Further, we have a set of epistles written by the most eminent of all the Apostles of Christ, who became a Christian after His Master's death. Four of these epistles — those to the Galatians and the Romans, and the two to the Corinthians — are admitted by all reasonable critics, believers and unbelievers, to be the genuine productions of the man whose name they bear; and these four bear abundant testimony to all the main facts of the life and teaching of our Lord, so that, if the whole early literature of the Christian Church had perished, or were to be lost or discredited, we could reconstruct from these admittedly genuine documents the whole Christian system.

These are the documents which we have now to examine with the view of discovering what proofs they afford of the resurrection of Jesus Christ from the dead. And in doing so we naturally ask two questions: (1) What did the disciples of Jesus Christ believe and assert? and (2) Does their belief justify us in believing in the resurrection of their Master? or is there any other theory more consistent with the facts of the case, viewed in the light of reason and experience? This is really the whole question which we have to consider; and we now proceed to examine, first, the testimony of the Gospels, and secondly, the testimony of Saint Paul, especially as it is contained in the fifteenth chapter of the First Epistle to the Corinthians.

4. THE EVIDENCE OF THE GOSPEL HISTORIES.

It is hardly necessary to say that we are here concerned with the Gospel narratives merely as credible history. For our present purpose we have no concern with the question of their inspiration, nor even of necessity with their authorship, but only with their internal coherence and consistency. We have before us a series of historical documents professing, among other things, to give an account of the resurrection of Jesus Christ from the dead, and of His appearance to His disciples after His resurrection; and we have to ask whether these accounts are contradictory and incredible, or whether they present such variations only as might be expected in writers giving an independent account of the same events, each one relating those facts with which he was best acquainted, in which he was most deeply interested, and which he regarded as best adapted for his purpose.

And here we naturally ask, What amount of agreement between historians is necessary in order to secure belief in their veracity or accuracy? What amount of discrepancy, real or apparent, is compatible with the truth of the main facts attested? On this point we are willing to take the judgment of an adversary.

"It may fairly be said," remarks Mr. Macan,[1] "if various persons report one event or series of events, we do not expect entire harmony and agreement in the details of their narratives; still less should we form such expectations in the case of supernatural events, supposing the latter to have really occurred. . . . One of the grounds of belief or disbelief," he goes on, "is the agreement or disagreement of various witnesses with each other and with themselves; a certain amount of disagreement and inconsistency may not invalidate their testimony, may even allay the suspicion of possible fraud or collusion: but there is some limit to be observed in this matter; there is a point where divergence becomes as suspicious as complete harmony, and where inconsistency becomes inconsistent with truth." With this general statement of the case we have no fault to find; and we must now ask whether the testimonies of the Gospels be credible, as presenting neither evidence of collusion by a suspicious resemblance,

[1] Essay, pp. 34, 35.

nor proof of untrustworthiness by manifest contradictions and inconsistencies.

What is quite clear is this,—that all the four Evangelists assert unhesitatingly that Jesus did actually rise from the dead; or, in detail, that He actually died on the cross and was laid in the grave, that afterwards the grave was found empty, and that subsequently He was seen alive by the Apostles and others before He disappeared from the earth. What objections are alleged against these accounts? We take the weightiest of them as they appear in the latest polemics of unbelief.

First of all, it is pointed out that no one actually saw Jesus come out of the grave; then, that the different Evangelists disagree as to the time when the women came to the sepulchre, as to the number of the women, as to the order of the appearances, and the places in which our Lord appeared to His disciples. It is also said that some of the details are legendary, and that the acts attributed to the risen Saviour are inconsistent and contradictory.

Certainly, to go no further, we have here a serious array of difficulties; and when they are thus stated nakedly, they seem almost insuperable. When, however, we view them more closely, their importance will be found to diminish; some of them will seem very trifling indeed, others will give way to a little patient examination, and some which are less easily brought into harmony may yet be shown to offer no real difficulty in the way of belief, since hypotheses of sufficient probability may be suggested for their reconciliation.

Let us consider the apparent difficulties in order. (1) There was no actual witness of the Resurrection itself, we are told. The author of "Supernatural Religion" thinks this fact so important that he brings it forward more than once.[1] A very simple illustration will show the exact value of this objection. You see a friend in bed asleep. You leave his room and come back after a certain interval, and you find the bed empty. Shortly afterwards you meet him in the street and speak to him. You did not see him get out of bed; but you are as sure of the fact as though you had seen him rise. Even Mr. Macan allows that "the evidence on which the Apostles believed was almost as strong as it could have been had they seen Jesus leave the tomb, as they had a few days before seen Lazarus come forth." Perhaps this is enough; but we shall have to refer to the objection again when we come to consider the theories invented to neutralize the value of the evidence in behalf of the Resurrection.

(2) As regards the time when the women came to the sepulchre, Saint Matthew says it was "late on the Sabbath day, as it began to dawn toward the first day of the week." Saint Mark says, "very early on the first day of the

---

[1] Supernatural Religion, vol. iii. pp. 484, 485; Macan, p. 28.

week . . . when the sun was risen." Saint Luke says, "on the first day of the week at early dawn." Saint John, "on the first day of the week, . . . while it was yet dark" (Revised Version). Now the presumed contradiction is this, that Saint John says it was yet dark, and Saint Mark says the sun had risen; but Mr. Macan, who points out this apparent discrepancy,[1] does not note the phrase employed by Saint Matthew, "as it began to dawn," which exactly reconciles the two other statements, and is the more remarkable as it is connected with the expression in which this Evangelist stands alone, "late on the Sabbath day," or, as in the Authorized Version, "in the end of the Sabbath." Mr. Macan actually bases on the language of Saint Matthew the theory that this Evangelist regarded the Resurrection as having taken place on what we should call the Saturday evening, although it is he and he alone who tells us that it was beginning to dawn. Two things we will venture to say respecting the various expressions employed by the four Evangelists, — that a really thoughtful reader would obtain very nearly the same idea of the time of the visit to the sepulchre from any one of the Gospels, and yet the phraseology is so remarkably distinct as to give the clearest evidence of independence. A greater proof of accuracy as well as truthfulness we should find it difficult to imagine.

[1] Essay, p. 39.

(3) There is much greater difficulty about the number of the women and the order of the appearances of Jesus after His resurrection. According to Saint John, Mary Magdalene came to the sepulchre; according to Saint Matthew, the two Marys; according to Saint Mark, the two Marys and Salome came; according to Saint Luke, several women, including the two Marys and Joanna. Further, according to Saint Mark and Saint John, the first appearance was to Mary Magdalene. According to Saint Matthew, it was to the women that He appeared, although he does not speak of it as the first appearance.

Now, are these statements necessarily contradictory? They certainly are not identical; and this is the best proof of their independence, and of the sincerity of the writers. But it is not impossible to weave a connected narrative out of the statements of the different Evangelists, which shall be perfectly coherent and harmonious, and yet shall omit no point which they record.

Let us note then, first of all, that, although Saint John uses language which seems to imply that Mary Magdalene came alone to the sepulchre, he incidentally shows that she was not alone, for he represents her as saying, "We know not where they have laid Him." If, then, we suppose that several of the women came together to the sepulchre, and that Mary Magdalene was separated from them for a short time,

— a thing which might quite easily happen in the gray dawn of the morning, — we can quite understand that our Lord showed Himself to her first, and that He appeared directly afterwards to the other women, as recorded by Saint Matthew, who gives the fact generally without reference to the circumstance (with which, perhaps, he was not acquainted) that He had first appeared to Mary Magdalene by herself.

It has been remarked that while Saint Luke tells us of an appearance to Simon Peter, Saint John, who was his companion, says nothing of the matter. But here we have a remarkable confirmation of the truth of his narrative; for it appears that the two disciples had separated before the Lord appeared to Simon, and we know it is the custom of Saint John to record only those events in which he took part himself, or else those which were necessary for the explanation of events which he witnessed and recorded.[1] In all probability, as we shall see later on, Saint Luke obtained the information respecting the appearance to Peter from Saint Paul.

Again, it is said that Saint Matthew records no appearances of our Lord to the disciples in Jerusalem, Saint Mark and Saint Luke none in Galilee. Yet Saint Luke says that the angels

---

[1] This characteristic of the fourth Gospel has been brought out very clearly by recent commentators, as Luthardt, Godet, and Westcott.

reminded them of what the Saviour had said while He was in Galilee, without adding the promise of His appearing there, inasmuch as he did not mean to record that manifestation; while Saint Matthew, for the opposite reason, may have preserved the words in which the angels told the women that the Lord was going into Galilee; and Saint John records appearances both in Jerusalem and in Galilee.

There are some other minor difficulties, on which no great stress can be laid, such as the account of the anointing, the number of the angels, and some other points. But of what use would it be to discuss the number of the angels at the sepulchre, when the author of "Supernatural Religion" regards the mere introduction of an angel at all as a proof of the unhistorical character of the narrative? "Can we believe," he asks, "that an 'angel,' causing an earthquake, [where is that asserted?] actually descended and took such a part in this transaction?" And then he adds, "If the introduction of the angel be legendary, must not also his words be so?"[1]

Yes; but why should the "introduction of the angel be legendary"? If it were so, the critic would still have to deal with the appearances of Christ to His disciples; he would still have to account for their belief in the resurrection of their Lord. But what necessity is there for suggesting the theory of legend? If an

[1] Supernatural Religion, vol. iii. pp. 448, 449.

event so stupendous as the Resurrection took place, it was by no means incredible that it should be witnessed by angels. The opposition to these details of the miracle really rests upon the supposition that the Resurrection could not have taken place, or did not take place. But this is to beg the whole question; and it will be found that the main objections urged against this portion of the Gospel narrative are, for the most part, of a purely *a priori* character.

Difficulties and apparent contradictions, such as are here met with, would present no real obstacle to belief if they were found connected with ordinary human history. It is the assumption that the main narrative in this case *cannot* be true, which leads to the exaggeration of the difficulties in the details of the history. It is impossible to resist the conviction that the objectors to the truth of the Resurrection find discrepancies in the history because they have made up their minds that they are not to believe it.

Besides the points already noticed, two or three of minor importance should at least be mentioned. Thus it is said that the beautiful and touching narrative of our Lord's appearance to the two disciples on the way to Emmaus is essentially legendary.[1] But this is the very point in question,—the very thing which has to be proved and not to be assumed. The writer

---

[1] Supernatural Religion, vol. iii. p. 462.

might with as much propriety tell us at once that the whole history is legendary, and have done with it. We cannot accept his prejudice or his impression as proof of the unhistorical character of an incident which the Christian regards with gratitude and delight, and which can be set aside only on grounds that would be fatal to all religion as well as revelation.

Then the same writer tells us, with the greatest confidence, that, if the risen Jesus could eat a piece of broiled fish, He could not enter a room when the door was closed, nor vanish suddenly out of the sight of His disciples;[1] but this is assuming a knowledge of the properties of matter to which the most learned of scientific men will make no pretensions.

Once more, it is alleged that the accounts of the Ascension are contradictory and irreconcilable. Saint John does not mention it. Saint Mark records the fact without saying where it happened. Saint Matthew seems to say it took place in Galilee. Happily, however, for the credit of the Evangelists, the principal objector to the historical character of their work does not merely accuse them of contradicting each other; he accuses Saint Luke of contradicting himself. In the Gospel, he says, Saint Luke represents the Ascension as taking place on the same day as the Resurrection, and in the Acts of the Apostles (for he allows that both books are

[1] Supernatural Religion, vol. iii. p. 459.

from the same hand) he says it was forty days later.[1]

It is a very happy example of the unreasonable and captious temper in which these documents have been examined. If these two books were by different writers, we should certainly be told triumphantly that there was a manifest discrepancy between them. Seeing that they are by the same writer, the second book taking up the narrative at the point at which the earlier dropped it, there would certainly be needed a great stretch of credulity to believe that the first page of the second part flatly contradicted the last page of the first. Surely, the natural explanation is much simpler and more credible. In the Gospel Saint Luke recorded the bare fact, and in the Acts he gave it in its connection with other events. It is a good illustration of the difference between the more condensed and the more extended narratives of the sacred books. The writers are frequently careless of the indications of place or time, where these would have no significance for the contents of their record. When they seem essential, they are mentioned. In the Acts of the Apostles, Saint Luke was about to record the descent of the Holy Spirit, and therefore he speaks of the lengthened period of preparation for that great event which our Lord afforded to His disciples. In the Gospel He was recording the history of parts of the life

[1] Supernatural Religion, vol. iii. pp. 470, 474, 571.

and work of Christ, and he simply added the mention of His ascension to the account of His resurrection. An explanation so simple of the seeming contradictions between two works of the same writer may serve to render us cautious in believing that one of these writers contradicts another.

What would be the verdict in a court of justice, if evidences such as we possess of the resurrection of Christ were brought forward on behalf of any event to which the witnesses could bear personal testimony? Even if the seeming discrepancies in their witness were real discrepancies, no reasonable man would doubt as to the truth of the main fact. In certain details, they would say, there may have been slight failures of memory, but as regards the central fact there can be no room for doubt.

And this is the conclusion arrived at even by rationalistic writers who have examined the evidences of the resurrection of Jesus. Even although the particular facts in the history, says Keim,[1] be contradictory and legendary, " the resurrection of Jesus in general " — the Resurrection itself, that is to say — " belongs to the most certainly proved facts of the New Testament." We see no reason to infer a legendary character in any part of the record; we certainly are not sensible that any of the seeming discrepancies must be understood to be contradictions; but

[1] Geschichte Jesu von Nazara, vol. iii. p. 529.

we gladly accept the testimony and assert the truth, that the resurrection of Jesus Christ from the dead is most surely proved and established to the satisfaction of the most critical investigator who is willing to give its true force to the evidence adduced.

5. THE EVIDENCE OF SAINT PAUL.

In dealing with the evidence of Saint Paul for the Resurrection we have this peculiar advantage, that we are occupying ground which is not seriously contested. Many of the recent assailants of Divine Revelation deny the authenticity of our Gospels on internal grounds, either attributing to them an origin more recent than is consistent with their reputed authorship, or else asserting that the original documents have been overlaid by later additions.

In regard to the history and the writings of Saint Paul, the case is different. The broad facts of his history are not denied; the genuineness of certain of his writings is not contested. We are, therefore, on ground which is allowed by our adversaries; and the only question between us has regard to the true significance of Saint Paul's testimony, and its bearing upon the reality of the resurrection of our Lord. Let us begin, then, by stating the points on which there is general agreement among all reasonable students of this subject.

It is agreed that a man whose original name was Saul, a native of Tarsus, lived at the time to which his history is assigned, about the middle of the first century of our era; that he was originally an earnest or even a fanatical Jew; that he was a persecutor of the disciples of Jesus, — those who were called Christians or named contemptuously Nazarenes. It is agreed that this persecutor was himself converted to a belief in Jesus Christ, and that he became, in consequence, the most zealous and devoted preacher of the faith he had once sought to destroy. Under his new name of Paul he traversed considerable portions of the Roman Empire, preaching the Gospel, founding churches, guiding the infant communities which his teaching had called into existence; and finally he died a witness for the faith which he had proclaimed. It is not denied that he made the greatest sacrifices for the faith which he preached, or that he was induced to change the whole current and purpose of his life by an undoubting belief that Jesus Christ had risen from the dead. So much is conceded by all who are worthy of consideration in this controversy.

In order to ascertain the value of this testimony for ourselves, we must find out what is the nature of the documents in which it is handed down to us; and then, by a careful examination of those documents, consider what convictions must be wrought in our own minds by the testimony which they afford. That we may avoid all needless distraction from our main purpose, we shall restrict ourselves to those documents the genuineness of which is not disputed. We shall, therefore, make no use, except incidentally, of the Acts of the Apostles, nor of the disputed epistles of Saint Paul.

Now, there are at least four epistles which, as M. Renan remarks,[1] are "incontestable and uncontested,"— the Epistle to the Galatians, the two Epistles to the Corinthians, and the Epistle to the Romans. M. Renan himself believes that several others are Saint Paul's; but these are allowed by the whole critical school of Tübingen, and they are sufficient for our purpose. Let us see what we may learn from them concerning the resurrection of Christ.

Now, at a glance we see two things: first, that Saint Paul was converted by having received, as he believed, in some way, a revelation of Jesus Christ, — that he believed himself to have actually beheld the risen Lord, and that he had learned from many other Christians that they also had seen Him after His resurrection; and further, that many of those who had seen Him were alive at the time when the Apostle wrote. These general statements cannot possibly be called in question; but it is necessary to examine them more carefully in order to ascertain what basis they afford for our belief, and

[1] Saint Paul, Introduction, part v. See Note II.

whether it is possible to suggest any hypothesis different from that of the actual resurrection of Christ, which will account for the undenied and undeniable facts now recounted.

First, let us remark that we have here a perfectly independent testimony. It is not a mere summary of the Gospel narrative made by a compiler or condenser of older documents. It is not pretended that any of the facts to which Saint Paul bears testimony were derived from the written books of the Evangelists, or from any similar records or histories. He gained them either from the revelation of Jesus Christ, or from the living men who were his own contemporaries, friends, fellow-workers. Even if it could be proved that the accounts of the Resurrection contained in the Gospels are legendary and contradictory, which we do not believe, the independent testimony of Saint Paul, and of those who were alive when he wrote, must be dealt with on its own merits.

Let us begin with Saint Paul's assertion of the appearance of the risen Lord to himself. In the Epistle to the Galatians[1] he says, "It pleased God to reveal His Son in me." We have no doubt the reference here is to the manner of his conversion as it is three times recorded in the Acts of the Apostles. As, however, we are using no authorities outside the limits of the uncontested Epistles, we will concede that this

[1] Gal. i. 15, 16.

statement might signify no more than a revelation of Christ to the heart and spirit of the Apostle. The same, however, cannot be said of the passage in the fifteenth chapter of the First Epistle to the Corinthians. Here, after enumerating a series of appearances of the risen Jesus, he adds, " Last of all He was seen of me also."[1] And in another place[2] he asks: " Have I not seen Jesus our Lord?"

Saint Paul then asserts that he had seen the Lord Jesus after His resurrection, just as the others had seen Him. It does not follow, as some critics have insinuated, that all the previous appearances had been of precisely the same character as that which was granted to him, who was as one born out of due time; but simply that he also did see the Lord, and had no doubt of that fact.

Several points in connection with this appearance will have to be considered when we come to examine the theories by which it has been attempted to set aside the evidences for the Resurrection as a whole. At present we are simply considering the value of Saint Paul's testimony as trustworthy evidence. Now, the value of this particular testimony by itself will depend greatly upon the character, circumstances, and conduct of the man by whom it is borne. And, happily, these are well known. We know what kind of man Saint Paul was. We know whether he was

[1] 1 Cor. xv. 8. [2] 2 Cor. ix. 1.

a man likely to take up a change of opinion lightly, whether his was one of those illogical minds, full of fancies and imaginations, which would mistake its own internal sensations for objective facts. Saint Paul was a highly educated Hebrew, thoroughly acquainted with the religion of his fathers, and bitterly opposed to the Gospel of Christ. It is quite conceivable that before the time of his conversion doubts may have passed through his mind, but they had not lodged there. He had heard the testimony of the Apostles. He had listened to the defence of the first martyr, Saint Stephen, and had given his vote[1] for his death. He had witnessed his martyrdom. Yet he was in no wise turned from his purpose, and still went on " breathing out threatenings and slaughter against the disciples of the Lord." [2]

Various theories[3] have been invented to account for the undeniable fact of the conversion of Saul of Tarsus. It has been suggested that his conscience had become so troubled by the thought of his cruelty towards the Christians, that he was prepared to interpret almost any startling event as a sign of a divine interposition; that he was probably alarmed by a thunderstorm while engaged in the work of persecution, and then imagined that something took place like that which is recorded in the

---

[1] This seems to be the meaning of ψῆφον.
[2] Acts ix. 1. [3] See Macan, p. 83.

Acts of the Apostles; and that then, under the influence of this new sentiment thus enkindled, he began to burn with an enthusiasm which left him no time for reflection on the nature of the evidence which had satisfied him of the resurrection of Christ.

And this is the theory which we are expected to receive in place of the clear and consistent account of the matter which is given three times in the New Testament by one who was undoubtedly the companion of Saint Paul! It is, of course, easy enough to invent any number of theories, and those who are determined to believe in no supernatural facts are driven to these straits; but those who are under no such necessity may be permitted to judge of such theories as infinitely more difficult of belief, more unnatural, and more unreasonable than the simple story of the New Testament.

In the writings of Saint Paul we certainly meet with no trace of such influences as are here supposed. He was perfectly sincere in his hatred of the Gospel and of Jesus of Nazareth. What he did against Him and His disciples he did ignorantly, in unbelief. On this point his own Epistles and the Acts of the Apostles are in entire agreement. Saint Paul evidently believed that, until it pleased God to reveal His Son in him, he was in darkness, in error, and in sin. He evidently believed that it was this revelation which produced the change in him, and not his own mental agitation which made him look upon some natural phenomena as signs of the presence of Christ.

Is there any reason, from what we know of Saint Paul's subsequent conduct, to suppose that he was seized by a sudden impulse which prevented his rationally investigating the causes of his conversion? Did he go forth on his work heedless of other men's testimonies to the Master, to whose service he now, once for all, consecrated his life? We have no doubt that Saint Paul was thoroughly convinced,[1] by the events which accompanied his conversion, that he had seen the Lord; that Jesus, whom he was persecuting, had actually appeared to him. In the Epistle to the Galatians he distinctly tells us that he received his commission and the Gospel which he preached immediately from Christ.

Now, we must confess that if Saint Paul had simply acted upon this conviction, without any communication with the other Apostles, as far as we are concerned, his testimony would have been of less value. But that was not the case. In that great chapter of the First Epistle to the Corinthians, in which he teaches the resurrection of the dead, he brings forward a series of testimonies to the resurrection of Christ which

---

[1] We are here in complete agreement with the author of "Supernatural Religion" (vol. iii. p. 494), who says that "Paul was quite satisfied with his own convictions;" although we deny his inference from that fact.

his readers might verify for themselves. Surely, this is not the work of a mere enthusiast, but of a calm, thoughtful, reasonable man. We must draw special attention to these testimonies, because they are of the greatest possible value, and the impugners of the truth of the Resurrection have felt that here they must put forth the whole strength of their attack if they would hope to destroy the Christian faith.

The first objection alleged is the most extraordinary. It is to the effect that " the testimony upon which the Resurrection rests," is " comprised in a dozen lines"![1] But what is the testimony the worse for its brevity? The real question to be considered is its truth or its falsehood, and the means which the witnesses had of knowing whether it was true or not.

Then, it is said, there can be no doubt " that Paul intended to give the appearances in chronological order," and that it would " be a fair inference that he intended to mention all the appearances of which he was aware."[2] We know of no reason for allowing the truth of either of these assertions; but if they were true they could not in the least degree affect the value of the testimonies actually given.

Two things are quite obvious: first, that Saint Paul obtained the testimony which he here records from the persons whom he mentions as

[1] Supernatural Religion, vol. iii. p. 483.
[2] Ibid., p. 488.

having seen the Lord after his resurrection; and secondly, that he put this testimony upon record at a time when the witnesses were alive, at a time when they themselves were proclaiming the same facts, and when it was possible and easy to interrogate them on the subject of their testimony. It is agreed that the Epistle was written between twenty and thirty years after the resurrection of Christ, when Saint Peter and most of the Apostles were alive; and the writer distinctly states that the greater number of those who had been witnesses remained "unto this present."[1]

The very selection of the instances which he places on record is significant; and it might suggest to a candid reader that these instances are not exhaustive. He mentions Peter and James as having seen the Lord; and it is noteworthy that these are the "pillar" Apostles whom alone he saw, as he tells us in the Epistle to the Galatians,[2] when three years after his conversion he went up to Jerusalem. What more natural than that these two Apostles should have told this new convert, this new witness to the Resurrection, of their own interviews with their risen Lord?

It has actually been attempted to throw doubt upon this testimony: the event is mentioned in the most "cursory" manner by Saint Paul and by no one else. Saint John does not mention it,

[1] 1 Cor. xv. 6. [2] Gal. ii. 9.

although he was Saint Peter's companion. But the probable reason of Saint John's silence, to which we have already referred, is passed over. Yet we are not without partial confirmations of the testimony, if such were needed. Although we are not at present using the contents of the Gospels, we may yet note, in passing, that Saint Mark, the companion of Saint Peter, records the words of the angel at the sepulchre, "Go tell the disciples and Peter,"[1] indicating a special reference to him; and Saint Luke,[2] the companion of Saint Paul, represents the Apostles as speaking of the Lord having "appeared unto Simon."

But indeed, as we have already hinted, the special mention of these two appearances by Saint Paul is in no way unnatural, but the reverse. As we have remarked, they were the two whom the Apostle first met after his conversion. It was hardly possible that they should omit to tell him of their having seen the Lord when they heard his testimony; and it was quite impossible that he should ever forget it. Will any one venture to suggest that Saint Paul put these testimonies on record, and that, too, during the life of the alleged witnesses, without having received their authority for the testimony?

But, further, Saint Paul tells us that the Lord appeared not to two only, but to the twelve, — that is, to the whole company of the Apostles, —

[1] Mark xvi. 7.   [2] Luke xxiv. 34.

and then to five hundred of the brethren, and lastly to himself. Even if these were all the appearances that the Apostle had heard of, the value of his evidence would in no way be lessened; but we cannot help being struck by the notion of there being a selection, when we consider the cases actually mentioned. And this may explain the omission of the appearances to Mary Magdalene and the other women. In those days women were not heard as witnesses in a court of justice; and the Apostle may have felt that their testimony would have added nothing to the proofs which he adduced in evidence of the Resurrection.

With regard to the appearance to the five hundred, it is objected that this occurrence is not mentioned in the Gospels.[1] Here is a specimen of the kind of criticism against which we have a right to protest in the name of science and consistency. First of all, the testimony of the Gospels is declared to be untrustworthy, and then it is brought in to cast doubt upon evidence which could not otherwise be discredited. If the defenders of the Gospel were as arbitrary in their method of handling their authorities, they would be loftily reminded that no treatment of these subjects could ever receive attention which was not conducted in a manner purely scientific! There is, however, nothing in the Gospels that would lead us to

[1] Supernatural Religion, vol. iii. p. 491.

doubt the truth of Saint Paul's statement about the appearance of the Lord to five hundred at one time, probably in Galilee. The Apostle's statement is precise, and seems to challenge investigation. Of these five hundred, he says, "the greater part remain unto this present." Nothing could be much easier than the verification of such an assertion. It was made with reference to events which did not concern merely a small and obscure body of men, but events which were openly proclaimed by a hundred voices in the light of day, events with which Syria and Asia Minor and Greece were ringing. If the Apostle could write words like these to the inhabitants of a city so distinguished for its philosophical culture as Corinth, without the distinct knowledge of their truth, he must have been either an impostor or a madman. Rather, he must have been both; and the worst enemies of the Gospel will hardly assert that he was either the one or the other.

What, then, is the inevitable conclusion at which we arrive from an investigation of this portion of Saint Paul's writings? Surely this, as it has been stated by a writer who is not favorable to Christianity,[1] "that within a few years of Christ's resurrection, a large number of people believed that he had risen from the dead,"

[1] Major Butler, author of "Erewhon," etc., in the "Fair Haven," p. 27.

and "that they had seen Him alive after He had been dead. This," he says, "has been well established, and indeed has seldom been denied."

Such, then, was the undoubting belief of the disciples of Jesus Christ. They were not, then, deceivers; they said what they believed to be true. Were they, then, deceived, were they mistaken in this belief? This is the only question which remains for consideration; and it shall receive attention in the closing Lecture.

LECTURE VIII.

THE RESURRECTION OF JESUS CHRIST.

PART II.

EXAMINATION OF THEORIES INVENTED TO SET ASIDE THE EVIDENCE FOR THE RESURRECTION.

No Evidence will convince those who are resolved not to believe. — Theory of Imposture abandoned. — How, then, escape from the Force of the Testimony? — Two Theories: 1. The Theory of Apparent Death, — partly abandoned, partly kept in Reserve. — The one Element of Probability in the Theory. — But consider what the Theory requires us to believe. — Difficulties. — Does not account for the Change in the Apostles. — Involves Imposture. — 2. The Vision Hypothesis. — The last Word of the Assailants. — Asserts Illusion, not Imposture. — The Theory explained. — Not entirely new. — Different Views of Strauss. — What the Illusion Theory involves. — Requires the inadmissible Assumption that the Disciples expected the Resurrection. — The Theory does not account for the Change in the Disciples. — Inconsistent Treatment of the Gospels. — Mary Magdalene. — The Apostles. — Their Doubts and Disbelief. — The Vision fails to account for undoubted Facts. — Why did the Appearances cease so abruptly? — What became of the Sacred Body? — The Truth of the Resurrection alone accounts for the new Faith of the Disciples. — The End of this Controversy.

IF the examination of the question of the resurrection of Jesus Christ from the dead were allowed to be a mere question of evidence, determined as any other matter of doubt would be, there certainly would appear to be no difficulty in arriving at a final conclusion. The evidence which satisfied the disciples of Christ might suffice for the convincing of any unprejudiced inquirer. But the assailant of the Gospel is not unprejudiced. He has resolved that he will believe in no supernatural occurrences; and therefore, if proofs that seem adequate are brought forward in support of such occurrences, it becomes necessary to invent some theory which shall account for the testimony without allowing the truth of the matter to which the testimony is borne.

So it has been with the resurrection of Christ. Its assailants are quite candid. They tell us that no evidence is conceivable that would prove it; and then they try to show that the evidence given is insufficient. We are now to consider whether any of the theories which they offer can be reasonably regarded as sufficient to set aside the evidence which we have already brought forward. There are only two or three of these theories which even the opponents of the Gospel would now think worthy of attention.

In the first place, there are few, if any, who will in these days even suggest that the first Christian teachers were impostors. This theory was a very early one. As we learn from Origen, it was advocated by Celsus; and it has been from time to time revived in the coarser forms of unbelief. Nay more, as we shall have to show, the assumption of imposture is more or less involved in one of the theories, which still possesses some adherents, although the advocates of the theory themselves do not consciously hold this opinion. In fact, there is in these days no assailant of the doctrine of the Resurrection of any eminence or respectability who thinks of charging the Apostles with imposture. Whether we consider the men themselves, or the doctrines which they promulgated, or the circumstances in which they were placed, we feel that, whatever they were, they were not deceivers; they could not have been conscious liars. Even if we knew nothing of their characters, even if we ignored the contents of their teaching, we must admit that they could have no motive for undertaking the ministry of the Gospel of Christ, except a strong faith in its truth, when they had only poverty and suffering and death as their earthly reward.

Unbelievers must, therefore, find other ways of escape from the force of their testimony than the charge of dishonesty. Two theories have accordingly been brought forward in recent times with the purpose of neutralizing the evidence for the Resurrection: the first, that Jesus did not really die, but was taken from the cross in a swoon, and afterwards revived; the second, that the disciples did not really see their risen Lord, but only imagined that they did. These theories we must now examine.

1. THE THEORY OF APPARENT DEATH.

With regard to the first of these suppositions, the theory that Jesus did not really die upon the cross, although it was advanced by Paulus and supported by some other writers of eminence, it may be said that it has been given up as untenable by the principal opponents of the Gospel,— for instance, by Strauss, Renan, Macan, the author of "Supernatural Religion," and others. As, however, it still has supporters of ability, and may yet be resuscitated if other theories have to be abandoned, it will not be safe to leave it unconsidered. The author of "Supernatural Religion," indeed, seems to keep it in reserve in case the "Illusion hypothesis" should prove a failure. "Although," he says, "we have no intention ourselves of adopting this explanation of the Resurrection, it is, as an alternative, certainly preferable to a belief in the miracle."[1] Not a very hopeful kind of controversialist, — one who starts with the assumption that, whatever may happen, the Resurrection cannot be believed! Any theory, however unreasonable, is to be accepted rather than this. We must leave the spectator of the fray to form a judgment respecting this attitude on the part of one of the combatants. It is for us, at any rate, to consider whether, "as an alternative,"

[1] Supernatural Religion, vol. iii. p. 485. Compare pp. 435, 446.

this theory be at all "preferable to a belief in" the Resurrection.

Now, the one element of probability which is contained in the theory of apparent death, is the fact that there was no actual proof that our Lord was really dead when He was taken from the cross. Whether subsequent occurrences did not afford proof ample and irresistible, whether any other supposition than that of his actual death can possibly be entertained,— these are questions which cannot be left out of consideration. It has, however, been urged with some force by scientific men, that there was no proof, at the time, that life had actually departed from the Body which was taken down from the cross. When, however, we consider what a doubt on this subject, or a denial of the actual death of the Lord Jesus, necessarily involves, then we can feel little difficulty in rejecting the theory.

For — let us mark it well — what this theory requires us to believe is this, that the appearances of the risen Saviour were those, not of one who had come forth from the grave in the fulness of a new life, but of a half-dead man who had crept from the tomb, after awaking from a deep and deathlike swoon; and that these appearances wrought an entire revolution in the faith and hope of the disciples of Jesus. Even the most resolute unbelievers in the Resurrection have felt constrained to reject this theory;

and before urging certain objections of our own, we will allow the critics of unbelief to give their judgment.

Mr. Macan [1] thus pronounces upon the theory in question: "It was very obvious to say that the glorious appearances of the risen Jesus were as unlike as possible to the comings and goings of a feeble convalescent, or of an invalid, who shortly sank again under the hardships which he had sustained; it was very obvious that such a mere convalescence could never have restored and transfigured the faith of the disciples, as it is generally admitted their faith was transfigured after the crucifixion. This rationalism is to us now-a-days but as a clumsy blunder." These remarks of Mr. Macan are little more than a repetition of the criticism offered by D. F. Strauss in his later work, to which the English writer is in many ways greatly indebted. "This view of the resuscitation of Jesus," says Strauss,[2] "apart from the difficulties. in which it is involved, does not for a moment solve the problem with which it is concerned, to explain the founding of the Christian Church as the result of a belief in the miraculous revivification of Jesus the Messiah. It is impossible that a being who had crept half dead out of the grave, and had crawled about in a state of weakness, needing surgical treatment,

[1] Essay, pp. 61, 62.
[2] Das Leben Jesu für das deutsche Volk, p. 298.

bandaging, strengthening, nursing, and who at last succumbed under his sufferings, should have given to his disciples the impression that he was the Conqueror of death and the grave, and the Prince of Life, — an impression which lay at the foundation of all their future testimony. Such a revivification could only have weakened the impression which he had made upon them in life and in death."

We submit that these difficulties are unanswerable. Such a theory does in no way account for the acknowledged fact of a marvellous change which was wrought in the mental condition of the disciples, — a change which led to the foundation and expansion of the Church of Christ upon earth. With such a criticism we might be contented to leave this theory. As, however, it has been revived in the book bearing the title of the "Fair Haven," already mentioned, it may be proper to point out that there are other and even more serious objections to the hypothesis in question.

Thus, the moment that we face the theory, we are confronted with questions like the following: "Did Jesus Himself profess to have risen from the dead, when He had only recovered from a swoon? And did His disciples, knowing the truth of the matter, represent His resuscitation as a resurrection wrought by the power of God?"

There are no consistent answers to such questions, and there is no agreement among the advocates of the theory as to what became of Jesus. According to one, He lingered on for a little while and then died. Another thinks that, like Moses, He withdrew Himself from the eyes of His followers, and died, probably on the Mount of Olives, hidden by a cloud from the eyes of His disciples. According to another He lived for a long time in an obscure quarter of Jerusalem, and sometimes in out-of-the-way parts of Galilee, showing Himself at rare intervals to His disciples. One writer [1] supposes that He lived for seven and twenty years after His crucifixion, and labored for the good of man. Some of these writers have suggested other theories which we do not here mention, lest we should be supposed to bring them forward for the mere purpose of casting ridicule upon the school from which they have proceeded.

It is quite unnecessary to criticise these theories in detail. There is one general consideration which must certainly be regarded as fatal to any form of the theory which holds that the death of Jesus was not real, but only apparent. Let us endeavor to make this consideration quite plain. The nature of our Lord's return to life — whether it was the resuscitation of one who had been half dead, who had been buried in a swoon, or a resurrection to life of one who had been really dead — must have been made

[1] Andreas Brennecke, quoted by Keim, vol. iii. p. 574.

known to those who had intercourse with Him after His resurrection. And even if, for a time, there might exist a doubt as to the nature of the change which had passed upon Him, that doubt would be entirely removed by His subsequent history. If He were merely a man brought back from a swoon, then He must have lived as other men lived, He must have eaten and drunk, and He must have taken rest in sleep; and this must have been known to friends or to foes. If it were known to foes, we are by this theory asked to believe that the enemies of the Christian Society allowed the Apostles to bear testimony to the resurrection of their Lord without making known the real facts of the case, which would forever have put an end to any belief in the assumed miracle. If it were known to His friends, then they were nothing short of impostors; for they gave out that He was not only risen from the dead, but that He had ascended to the right hand of God. This statement, let it be remembered, is not in the Gospel history only. It occurs repeatedly in the writings of Saint Paul: "It is Christ that died," he says, "yea rather, that is risen again, who is even at the right hand of God."[1]

We do not dwell upon the offensive suggestion — which, however, is quite inevitable, if we adopt this theory — that the Holy One Himself participated in the fraud.

[1] Rom. viii. 34.

It has already been remarked that there are few who will now put forward this explanation of the appearances of our Lord to His disciples after His death. We should not have regarded it as worthy of serious refutation but for the circumstance already noted, that it has still at least one advocate of some ability, and that the author of "Supernatural Religion" has indicated a disposition to fall back upon it, if his own hypothesis should be found wanting. We repeat, therefore, that in no respect does this theory account for the acknowledged facts or accord with them. It explains nothing, and is burdened with improbabilities and contradictions.

Some of the objections which may be urged against this theory are equally applicable to the one which has still to be examined. We refer in particular to the question of what became of the sacred Body of the Lord. We will, in conclusion, urge only one consideration which has already been noticed, and one which seems to be utterly fatal to its claims. If this hypothesis be true, it is impossible to acquit the first preachers of the Gospel of the charge of imposture. Their testimony was false, and they must have known it to be false. And this is what we are asked to believe. These impostors were the men who counted not their lives dear to them, but gave up all that the world had to give to them, that they might preach truth and righteousness and love and mercy to their fellow-men. In the propagation of these doctrines they endured the greatest sufferings willingly, joyfully. In testimony of the truth which they proclaimed, many of them died without a murmur, without a reproach addressed to Him who had called them to their work, without a doubt or a fear with respect to the hope which He had set before them. If there is a man on earth who can believe this, then certainly the belief of any miracles, however astounding, can be a matter of small difficulty. It is impossible for us to give credit to this implied charge of imposture. It is not believed by the adversaries of the Gospel themselves.

2. THE VISION HYPOTHESIS.

The theory which remains for consideration must be examined with the greatest attention, inasmuch as it may be said to be the last word of the assailants of the historical reality of the resurrection of Jesus Christ. It is not a new theory, and the fluctuations of unbelief on the subject may well give rise to reflections in a candid mind. It is quite clear that there is no small difficulty in getting over the numerous and weighty evidences which are alleged in support of the truth of our Lord's resurrection from the dead. Theories invented to account for the acknowledged facts of early Christian history have been put forward, tested, found wanting, and discarded. We do not say that they must therefore all, of necessity, be false; but it certainly raises a just suspicion that none of them may be true. The theory now to be considered, known as the Vision hypothesis, we hold to be no more satisfactory than that which assumed that our Lord was not dead, but only in a deep swoon, when He was laid in the grave; but it is more subtle, and the refutation of it requires a greater amount of critical attention.

The theory is sometimes spoken of as the Illusion hypothesis,—a term which more exactly describes its nature, inasmuch as a vision either may be subjective, or may involve the perception of an objective existence, of something which has a being independent of the percipient. We adopt the designation of "Vision hypothesis," however, as that which is most commonly employed,[1] and we proceed to say a few words on its nature and history.

According to the Vision hypothesis, our Lord did die, or probably did die, upon the cross; but He did not rise again, and He was not really seen alive after His burial. The disciples, however, thought that they saw Him on different occasions; and the belief that He had appeared, and therefore that He had risen from the dead, took such hold of them, and so spread among

---

[1] It is the term used by Strauss, the author of "Supernatural Religion," Mr. Macan, and others, and by Keim, who rejects it. Compare Note I.

them, that they held it as an undoubted fact, and proclaimed it as an essential part of the Gospel which they believed themselves commissioned to preach for the salvation of men.

The theory, as we have said, is not a new one, and its history is instructive. Something of the kind seems to have been held by Celsus, who is represented by Origen[1] as asking, "Who saw this [the Resurrection]? A half-frantic woman, as you say, and perhaps some one else addicted to the same kind of juggling, who had in some state dreamt it, or, in accordance with his own wish, by a wandering fancy, had imagined it." This is, in fact, very much the same as the modern Vision-hypothesis; but Celsus does not seem to have laid much stress upon it, for he adds, " or, which is more likely, one wished to impress others with this marvel ($\tau\epsilon\rho\alpha\tau\epsilon\acute{\iota}\alpha$), and by such a fraud to give occasion to other impostors."

It is noticeable that the theory did not gain wide acceptance among the assailants of the historical truth of the Gospel history. Paulus, the greatest of the rationalistic school, as we have seen, adopted the theory that Jesus had not died. Even Strauss, in his first "Life of Jesus," based purely upon the mythical theory, gave a somewhat different explanation of the Resurrection. The change in his views is indeed so significant in relation to the whole subject, that it

[1] Contra Celsum, ii. 55.

deserves to be noted.[1] In the earlier "Life" the explanation ordinarily given of the Gospel miracles amounted very much to this, that a large number of the contemporaries of Jesus expected that the Messiah would work a certain kind of miracles; and so, having attributed a Messianic character to Jesus, they came to believe that He actually did work such miracles. The idea generated the supposed facts. So, with regard to the Resurrection, the disciples, by reflection upon the Messianic idea, came to the conviction that the Soul of God must rise from the dead, and so to the belief that He actually had risen.

The success of this theory was, for a time, prodigious. It got rid of all the difficulties, many and great, of the rationalistic theory. It had an appearance of intellectual and spiritual elevation, which to many minds was very attractive and fascinating. It resolved the miraculous events of the Gospel history in a manner which promised to be final. It is not too much, however, to say that it has been, to a great extent, abandoned, and abandoned even by its inventor, or adopter, and most able and successful exponent, Dr. Strauss. Facts were at last too strong for his followers. It became clear that there were actual facts to be dealt with, which had certainly taken place, and

[1] This change has already been remarked in the first Lecture of the present series.

which could not be the mere product of ideas. Consequently, a theory must be found which would give a natural explanation of those facts; and this necessity led to a partial return to the rationalistic method. The events recorded in the Gospel must in a certain degree be accepted, but their miraculous character must be explained away. This new tendency found notable expression in Renan's "Vie de Jésus," published in 1863, and in Strauss's new "Life of Jesus for the German People," put forth in the following year.

The promulgation of the Vision hypothesis was one of the results and evidences of this change. Jesus was now recognized as a real personage of a great and elevated character, who had lived and taught, and exercised a powerful influence over the minds of His disciples, and who was put to death under Pontius Pilate. Those who had known Him in life came to believe that they had seen Him alive after His death. How could these supposed appearances be accounted for? They could not, of course, be regarded as real occurrences, as that would involve a belief in miracles which must be discarded. They must be regarded as imaginations, visions, hallucinations. Such is, in effect, the latest theory of Strauss, the theory of Renan, Macan, and the author of "Supernatural Religion."

Now, let us ask, fairly and candidly, what, on

this hypothesis, we are expected to believe. And first, what is its ground and starting-point? It is evidently to be found in the notion that the disciples expected their Master to rise again, and so persuaded themselves and each other that He had actually risen and that they had seen Him. It is a large demand to make upon our belief, — shall we say, upon our credulity? To most of us a larger demand than the requirement to believe in a miracle wrought by the power of God, and to accept the miraculous explanation of the resurrection of Christ as the best way of accounting for the acknowledged facts of history. We cannot pretend to approach the consideration of this theory with an expectation of finding it to be in any way credible.

In the first place, it is quite incredible that such a revolution should have been worked in the minds of the Apostles in the short space of three days. On this point there is no reason to doubt the general Christian belief. Saint Paul mentions that Jesus rose on the third day; and the institution of the first day of the week as the Lord's Day, which dates back to the earliest history of the Christian Society, is an abiding witness to that belief. We are asked, then, to believe that, in the short space of two days or less, the disciples had entirely changed their views of the character of the Messiah and His kingdom, and this without anything to account for it except what is called a natural reaction in their own minds!

Let us look at the facts. It is universally known and acknowledged that the disciples of Christ, like the mass of their countrymen, had very low and materialistic conceptions of the nature of the Messiah's kingdom. Saint Paul may be taken as an example, probably a favorable example, of the orthodox Jew, and as illustrating the views of such respecting Jesus of Nazareth. The death of Jesus naturally gave a great shock to those who held such views; and the writers who advocate the Vision hypothesis assert that, for a moment, their faith failed them. But directly afterwards — such is their theory — there was a reaction in their minds, and they not only recovered from their momentary doubts as to the Messiahship of Jesus, but conceived the belief that He must have risen again.[1]

The Gospel account is certainly far more reasonable, and much more in keeping with what we know of human nature and its laws. We know of no authority for the supposition that the disciples lost faith in their Master, in the sense of supposing that He had ever voluntarily misled them. But it is quite possible that they may have doubted whether they had rightly understood him when they thought He claimed to be the Messiah. That He was "a Prophet mighty in deed and word before God and all

[1] Macan, p. 85.

the people," they never had any reason to doubt; but they may quite naturally have entertained doubts of His being the promised King. The words of the disciples on the way to Emmaus contain a very natural expression of their thoughts: "We trusted that it had been He which should have redeemed Israel."[1]

How came it to pass that these men not only recovered their faith in the Messiahship of Jesus, but gained new and deeper and fuller views of the nature of His work, and a faith so strong that it never afterwards wavered? This is the real problem which we have to solve. Which is the more reasonable answer to this question, — that which is contained in the simple narrative of the New Testament, or these theories which are invented to explain away the meaning of that narrative?

The Gospel histories tell us, without any disguise, that the disciples were cast into a state of great doubt and fear by the death of their Master; and they further relate that their doubts and fears were dispelled by the sight of the empty tomb, and by repeated appearances of their risen Lord, which they had at first some difficulty in believing, but of which they afterwards became assured. The advocates of the Vision hypothesis, on the contrary, declare that the disciples spontaneously recovered from their dismay, conceived the idea of their Master's

---

[1] Luke xxiv. 21.

resurrection, and therefore came to believe in it, and to think they had seen Him alive.

These writers dwell with peculiar emphasis on the improbability of Saint John's account of the fears of the priests and the doubts of the disciples. Is it likely, we are asked, that the Jewish priests should have remembered a prophecy which Jesus had delivered respecting His resurrection, which His disciples had forgotten? Yes, we reply; both of these things are quite probable. Both were taught by their fears. When men's consciences are uneasy, they fear the worst. When men's hopes are shattered, they are slow to believe that they may yet be revived. Herod, when he heard of the fame of Jesus, thought that the murdered John must have risen from the grave; and the Jews had wickedly put to death a greater and a holier than John. Martha, the sister of Lazarus, was slow to understand the implied promise of her brother's restoration to life. "I know," she said,[1] "that he shall rise in the resurrection at the last day." The loss of the disciples was greater than hers, and their despondency deeper. And yet we are told — and the theory we are examining requires us to believe — that the Body of the Lord Jesus was hardly deposited in the tomb when they became assured that He would return, and then they immediately came to believe that He had returned, and that they

[1] John xi. 24.

had seen Him. Does not this look like an effect without any antecedent cause?

But we must not overlook the explanation which some have given of the dawning of this new hope within the hearts of the disciples. According to M. Renan,[1] it was "the powerful imagination of Mary of Magdala," which played the most important part in this transaction. She found the grave empty, and immediately her imagination took fire, and being raised up into a high state of enthusiasm, she took the first person that she met for the risen Master. "Divine power of love," exclaims M. Renan, "sacred moments in which the hallucination of an impassioned woman gives a resuscitated God to the world!"

Now, the history of the appearance of our Lord to Saint Mary Magdalene is a perfectly coherent one, and perfectly reasonable and intelligible, just as it stands. The moment that we try to make it say anything different from what it does say, we become involved in absurdities and contradictions. Say that it is fabulous, and that you do not admit its authority, and we will show that we are not dependent upon it. Or use it to prove that it was "a half-frantic woman" who produced a belief in the Resurrection among the disciples; but in that case take the story just as it stands on the pages of Saint John. Now, the history tells us that Mary

[1] Vie de Jésus, c. xxvi. p. 434.

Magdalene had no expectation that Jesus would rise. She came to the grave with spices to anoint His sacred Body. But she found the grave empty and the Body gone. Here at once we are told of something which accounts for her change of mind. Whether she remained to hear what the angels told the women, or whether she ran off at once to tell Saint Peter and Saint John of the empty grave, she had seen enough to prepare her for whatever might come.[1] But before we can believe that the reputed appearance of her risen Master was a mere vision or hallucination, we must have some account to give of the empty grave, and we must also satisfy ourselves that all the other appearances were imaginary, and not real. To the subject of the empty grave we will return presently. Let us first consider the effect which Mary's testimony had on the minds of the disciples.[2]

Did they at once accept the testimony that the grave was empty, that Mary had actually beheld its tenant restored to life again, and that therefore they might assure themselves that the Lord was risen? On the contrary, the conviction came to them gradually and slowly. These men were not all enthusiasts. Granting that there was among them a warm, impulsive Peter, there was also a cold and doubting Thomas. Were these the kind of men who, in a matter of

[1] Supernatural Religion, vol. iii. p. 497, note.
[2] Compare Macan, pp. 97, 101.

such vital importance, would catch at a floating rumor and immediately turn it into solid fact, and make it a fulcrum by means of which they would turn the whole course of their life into a new path, and move the world of thought and action? It is most improbable.

Saint Thomas was not the only one of whom we are told that he doubted. Saint Matthew[1] relates that, at the appearance in Galilee which he records, "when they saw Him they worshipped Him, but some doubted;" and the author of "Supernatural Religion" says the Evangelist has omitted " to tell us whether, and how, those doubts were set at rest."[2] But surely this is a rash statement, for the answer is really given in the very next verse: " And Jesus came and spoke unto them, saying, All power is given unto Me in heaven and in earth." Here was the resolution of their doubts, that He actually spoke to them, as He had been accustomed to do before His death; took up, as it were, and carried on the instructions which He had previously begun, enabling them to understand the meaning of His life and death, of His sufferings and His resurrection, as they could never before have understood them. But, apart from the narratives of the Evangelists, which are perfectly consistent on the supposition that there was an actual resurrection, followed by real appearances

---

[1] Matthew xxviii. 17.
[2] Supernatural Religion, vol. iii. p. 468.

of the risen One, the Vision hypothesis fails to explain certain undoubted facts in the apostolic history.

How came it to pass, we may ask, that there was such an entire agreement among the disciples as to the nature of these appearances? Let it be granted that a man in a high state of enthusiastic excitement may believe that he sees some object which is only the product of his own imagination. Let it be granted that such a man may communicate his own hallucination to others, so that they may come to believe that they have seen what he has seen, sometimes apart and singly, at other times when large numbers are assembled together. Even if we concede that this is possible, we cannot make the same concession when we are told that this illusion presented itself under the same form to all who had caught the enthusiasm, or that their testimony on the subject was completely harmonious and accordant.

There is another difficulty which lies in the path of this theory. If these appearances had no objective reality, how was it that they ceased so soon and so abruptly?[1] Why did they continue at intervals for a certain time to one after another, and to assemblies of the disciples, and then abruptly come to an end? If they were mere illusions begotten of a heated imagination, there was no reason why they should not

[1] This point is well urged by Keim.

continue. If we take the account of the matter which is given in the New Testament, all is clear and consistent. For forty days after His resurrection the Lord remained on earth, and manifested Himself from time to time to His disciples, speaking to them of the things pertaining to the Kingdom of God, and preparing them for the gift of the Holy Spirit. After His ascension He appeared only to Saint Stephen and to Saint Paul, and in a different manner afterwards to Saint John; but to all these "in glory." He had then ascended to the Father. Up to the time of His ascension He was in a certain sense personally present with His disciples on earth. From that time, and especially from the Day of Pentecost, He was still with them; but not in person. They had then another Comforter, even the Spirit of truth, who was appointed to abide with them, and lead them into all truth.

This is the account of the matter which is given in the New Testament, and it is quite clear and consistent. We understand the great change which took place at the end of the forty days. On the Vision hypothesis the change is totally inexplicable.

But there is still another question which requires an answer, and to which an answer must be given before either of these theories can be accepted as even worthy of consideration. "What became of the sacred Body which had been taken from the cross and laid in the grave?" Here at least there is agreement,— in the belief that Jesus Christ was crucified, and that He was buried. Whether He was only half dead and came to life again, or whether He was dead and did not revive, in either case He was at least buried, and in either case the sacred Body was ultimately deposited somewhere. On any theory opposed to that which asserts an actual resuscitation and resurrection, the question must be answered, What became of the Body of the Lord? Renan[1] treats this subject with his accustomed airy levity. " Had His body been taken away," he asks, " or was it an afterthought of enthusiasm, always credulous, which produced the stories, in order to establish faith in the Resurrection? . . . It is a matter," he adds, " in which, from the fault of contradictory documents, we shall be forever ignorant."

Others find "so many difficulties about the empty grave that even the fact has become suspect."[2] Perhaps, they urge, the body was still in the tomb. If so, it had probably become unrecognizable, and therefore it would have been of no avail to produce it. These considerations are actually brought forward as of weight. Let us be quite clear on one point. We are dealing here with a question in one sense sub-

[1] Vie de Jésus, p. 433 (1st French edition).
[2] Macan, p. 106.

ordinate, yet in another sense of no secondary importance. It is not fair or reasonable to treat it as of no moment. The actual disposal and destination of the sacred Body of the Lord have to be explained by any theory which professes to deserve credence; and the gravity of the subject has been felt from the earliest period. Tertullian tells us that many Jews in his day said that the gardener had removed it. Quite recently Réville suggests that Pilate may have got the soldiers to take it away, or that the members of the Sanhedrim may have removed it, and left the grave-clothes behind to prevent identification. One cannot help here noting, in passing, the implied belief that, after all, the stories in the Gospels are substantially true, and must be accounted for. Surely, this is the strangest way of explaining the empty grave, the body gone, and the grave-clothes left.

Let us, however, see that we appreciate the full importance of this question. Whatever the Jews may have believed or disbelieved with regard to the resurrection of Jesus, they were at least concerned to disprove it. They had put the Righteous One to death. There could be no more terrible proof of their wrong doing than the resurrection by divine power of Him whom they had slain. And now there were men speaking openly in Jerusalem, accusing them of the murder of the Messiah, and declaring that the Crucified One had risen from the grave.

What was the answer to this testimony? They might find difficulty in dealing with it as a whole. But on one point, at least, they could come to a decision. Either the Body was still in the grave or it was not. There was no attempt to produce it; so we may be quite sure it was not in the grave. Most certainly, sufficient time had not elapsed to prevent all possibility of identification. At least the pierced hands and side must have borne some trace of the wounds inflicted. There can be but one inference on this point. The Body was not produced because it was no longer in the grave.

Where was it? In the keeping of friends or in the hands of foes. Shall we say that the disciples had borne it away? This seems to have been one of the stories circulated by the Jews. But we have seen, over and over again, that such an account of the matter is incredible. If that were true, then the disciples were impostors, — a supposition which is now universally abandoned. But even this impossible theory will hardly support the notion. We have further to believe that a secret which must have been known to a large number of persons never leaked out, and that there was not one of them so honest, not one so indignant at the deception practised by his companions, as to expose their imposture. The theory breaks down at every point.

If, then, the Body of the Lord was not in the custody of His friends, can we believe that His enemies had stolen it from the tomb? How easily in that case might the controversy have been ended, and the testimony of the disciples refuted! They had only to produce the Body. They did not, simply because they could not. "He is risen; He is not here." That sacred form had, by the power of God, been raised from the three days' sleep, never to see death more. It is the only reasonable account of the matter. It is the one only theory which fully accounts for the facts which are not disputed by the adversaries of Christianity themselves.

We do not dwell upon the mighty results of the Resurrection as affording a proof of the reality of the occurrence. It is agreed on all hands that the Christian Church was founded upon this belief. Even if we were to admit that the belief was sufficient to account for those results quite apart from the objective reality of the things believed, we have yet to account for the origin of that new, victorious faith that sprang up within the hearts of the first preachers of the Gospel of Christ. Of this faith no reasonable account is given, or, we venture to think, can be given, apart from the reality of the resurrection of Christ by the power of God. The Vision hypothesis recognizes the existence and the power of this faith, and offers an explanation which really gives no help to the solution of the problem.

Like other theories, this one, we may safely predict, will have its day until its fallacy becomes so apparent that none will be found to avow it, and then it will take its place in the museum of the disused and useless artillery of unbelief. It has been already remarked that one of the latest advocates of the Vision hypothesis shows his doubts as to its sufficiency, by leaving it open for himself to take up anew the other theory which he had discarded. Rather, he says, than "fall back upon the hypothesis of a miracle, it would be preferable to adopt the theory of apparent death."[1] We are, therefore, doing no injustice to these controversialists when we say that they start with the determination not to believe in a miracle, and therefore with the fixed resolve to disbelieve in the resurrection of our Lord, whatever proofs or arguments may be brought forward in its support. We do not urge that such a method is profane and atheistical, because such charges would hardly disturb the complacency of our antagonists. We say it is unscientific and unreasonable. The existence of the Christian Church is a problem which cannot properly be dismissed in this manner; and those who refuse to admit the truth of that fact and doctrine upon which the Church has always professed to rest the

[1] Supernatural Religion, vol. iii. p. 524.

very foundation of her power, should at least be able to say that they had made a candid examination of the arguments brought forward in its support.

We have not followed cunningly devised fables, and we have no fear that any weapons formed against the city of God shall ever prosper. If, then, we feel constrained to contend earnestly for the faith once for all delivered to the Saints, it is not because we have any fear of its being overthrown. If we are forced to change the mode of our defence, it is not because we find any serious defects in the works of the Apologists who have gone before us ; it is because the failures of past attacks have compelled the assailants of the Gospel to adopt new methods of offence. We could afford to ignore these feeble attempts, knowing that they will soon be forgotten. But we must remember that there are many uninstructed and unskilful believers in Christ, whose peace may be disturbed, even if their faith is not destroyed, by hearing of objections to the faith to which no reply has been attempted. For their sakes — for the sake of the little ones who are dear to the heart of Christ, and for the sake of those who have but little time to give to the study of these difficulties, we must in the first place set forth the acknowledged facts of history, and in the second place vindicate their true meaning and significance ; having no fears for the Church of Christ, which can be overthrown no more than can the throne of the Eternal God, but believing that every fresh attack on the truth of the Gospel will, in the long run, conduce only to the strengthening of our faith.

NOTES.

NOTE A, *page* 28.

IT was about a century before this time that the writings of the English school of deists began to appear. Lord Herbert of Cherbury (1581–1648) is generally reckoned the first of them. But the chief men who gave distinct shape to their unbelief were Toland (1669–1722); Collins (1676–1729); Woolston (1669–1731); Tindal (1657–1733), author of "Christianity as old as the Creation," published in 1730, the work against which Butler's "Analogy" was principally directed; and Chubb (1679–1747). It was largely from the materials supplied by these writers that the Wolfenbüttel Fragments (*Wolfenbüttelsche Fragmente eines Ungenannten*) were composed. They were published by Lessing (1774–1778), who was then librarian at Wolfenbüttel, and were represented as being extracts from the library; but there is now no doubt that most of them were written by Hermann Samuel Reimarus (1694–1768), Professor of Hebrew in the Gymnasium at Hamburg. See Art. *Fragmente Wolfenbüttelsche*, in Herzog, *Real-Wörterbuch*, vol. iv. p. 597.

NOTE B, *page* 48.

Mr. Cotter Morison, in his recently published work on the "Service of Man" (London, 1887, pp. 13 *et seq.*), attempts to turn the edge of this argument, maintaining that the assailants of Christianity failed in former times because they were not furnished with the results of modern scientific inquiry. "Nothing is more common," he says, "than the assertion that any objections now made to Christianity are worn-out sophisms, which have been answered and disposed of over and over again." This is not quite our position, although such a rejoinder is not wholly unjustified. What we have here endeavored to show is, that the assailants of the Gospel have been beaten off in every successive attack, that they have been forced perpetually to change their ground and their methods of assault, and that every fresh change of method has resulted in discomfiture. Mr. Morison says that the defeat of the early deists and others by no means guarantees a victory over "the methods and results of modern science." To imagine such a thing "implies a complete misconception of the true bearings of the question under discussion." "The deists," he goes on, "were, to say the least, as unscientific as the theologians.... No blame attaches to the deists — able and worthy men most of them — for not transcending the knowledge of the age. They attempted prematurely to solve a problem before the means of solution were at hand."

Mr. Morison cannot settle the question in this offhand way. It remains, indeed, to be seen whether the present "scientific" attacks on the Gospel will be abandoned as the rationalistic and mythical methods have been. But at least the Christian apologists have given no signs of alarm in presence of this altered front. Their predecessors have beaten back the attacks of earlier assailants, and they do not doubt that they will be able to do the same with the present foes of the faith. Mr. Morison makes excuses for the unbelievers of the past, and implies that the new school will be more successful, because they will adopt methods more scientific. It does not seem to occur to him that the defenders of the Christian faith have also learnt something which may help them to be wiser and stronger in the fight. Indeed, it seems to be perpetually forgotten by the enemies of Christianity, that believers and unbelievers alike held the same opinions on scientific subjects in the past, and in this respect were equally liable to go astray. Christians, as such, had no opinions whatever on such subjects, and they are not, as Christians, responsible for the errors into which they fell. To make Christians in all ages responsible for old theories of "Genesis and Geology," or for peculiar theories of "Inspiration," not sanctioned by the Bible itself or by the Church at large, would be about as reasonable as to make scientific men in all ages responsible for the corpuscular theory of light.

NOTE C, *page* 77.

Since this lecture was written, the English Church Congress held at Wolverhampton (October, 1887) has been startled by hearing from Canon Isaac Taylor that Mahometanism is a better instrument for the civilization of Africa, at least, than Christianity. Such a statement has naturally drawn forth a good deal of criticism.

Into the allegations made by Mr. Taylor as regards the relative merits of African Christians and Mahometans it is not possible for us to enter. It is sufficient merely to note that, in certain particulars, the facts adduced by him are denied. It is more to our purpose to note that even Canon Taylor does not regard Mahometanism as on a level with Christianity. In a letter to the "Spectator" (Oct. 22, 1887), replying to some of his critics, he says: "I think Christianity immeasurably the higher and the better faith;" and he adds: "The cause, or one cause, of our failure is, I think, that our Christian standard is impractically high for degraded races." It is obvious, therefore, that whether Mr. Taylor is right or wrong, his views in no way come into conflict with the argument of this lecture.

One or two brief remarks may be added. We quite admit that a low form of religion or superstition may for a time be more easily diffused, and also, in a sense, more efficacious than a high and spiritual faith, although we should not feel justified in diffusing such a religion. In regard to Mahometanism, whatever excellences it possesses are in a great measure derived from Christianity itself, although it has little of the spirituality of the Gospel. With respect to the civilizing influences of the two religions in races which have come into contact with the Western nations, we may point to the Magyars and the Ottoman Turks. Both are of Turanian origin. The creed of Islam has stopped the progress of civilization in Turkey, while the Hungarians, who have for long been Christians, amalgamate freely with the Indo-European races, and are now hardly distinguishable from them. It will hardly be argued that the civilization of Turkey is on a level with that of Germany or of England.

NOTE D, *page* 115.

The reasons for omitting to notice the geological and other objections to the historical character of the Book of Genesis are various. In the first place, it seemed to me that the subjects actually treated were of greater present importance; and, besides, without entering upon other reasons, I must observe that the main arguments adduced in support of the truth of the Gospel in these lectures are entirely independent of any particular view of the Old Testament. On the general subject of the relation between the Bible and science, I am happy to express my concurrence with the following remarks of the Bishop of Bedford, contained in a sermon at Manchester Cathedral, England, preached in connection with the meeting of the British Association, Sept. 4, 1887.

He took for his text 2 Timothy iii. 16 (Revised Version), and said that while the Bible was profitable for teaching, for reproof, for correction, and for instruction in righteousness, he did not find that it claimed to be profitable for scientific study. The man of God was by it furnished completely unto every good work, but he did not discover that he was by it furnished even partially unto the conclusions of philosophic inquiry. He was quite sure that many needless difficulties had arisen from the prevalence of a narrow and mechanical view of inspiration, and that such difficulties would often be removed by a frank recognition of the truth that God allowed the writers of the Bible to write as men, each with his individuality distinctly impressed upon his work; each, while delivering God's message and guided by God's Spirit, using the ordinary phenomenal language of his day as to matters of science; and in no other way could such writer have been intelligible to his contemporaries. He was not made supernaturally acquainted with the mysteries of the universe or with the annals of universal history. People, therefore, should never go to the Bible for what it was never meant to teach. He supposed many in that congregation had been brought up in the old-fashioned belief, which seemed to our forefathers to rest so clearly on the authority of the Bible, that God created man upon the earth as a totally new and hitherto unknown being, essentially different from all other creatures, in full-grown stature and complete moral and intellectual development. But nobody was ignorant that modern speculations as to the origin of man were of a very different character from that old-fashioned belief. Of all those speculations the most prominent, as well as the most startling, was that propounded by the advocates of evolution. He was not sure that our best scientific men would hold that theory to be as yet established beyond question, but undoubtedly there were facts and arguments in its favor which it would be silly to despise, and which to a great number of persons, and to many of our scientific men, appeared to possess all but conclusive weight. Now, what was the Christian who believed in his Bible to say to all that? There were some devout men who would say that those and any such-like speculations were straight against God's Word, and were therefore untrue and absurd. But that was not the spirit which was likely to arrive at the truth. Had we so utterly forgotten the injury done to the cause of religion by the stolid resistance of the Church in former days to the discoveries of astronomy as opposed to the Bible? We had read the Bible wrongly before; we might be reading it wrongly now. He had called the language of the Bible upon physical matters phenomenal, because that language was obviously not meant to teach scientific truth or help scientific discovery, but was the language of appearances, describing things, as all popular language did, not as they are, but as they seem. If the writers of God's Word had been inspired to speak of things as they are in the truth of God's own knowledge, that mode of speaking would have been wholly unintelligible to man. In abstaining from scientific revelations, God's Word was simply adapting itself to our understandings, in the same way that it did when it spoke of God Himself, — in anthropomorphic language ascribing to Him the members of a human body, that we might see the shadow of His acts on the wall. But there was another attitude which some took up in regard to those speculations. They said that religion and science occupied wholly different spheres of Nature, and need in no way intermeddle with each other; they revolved, as it were, in different planes and never met. It was said we might pursue scientific studies with the utmost freedom and at the same time maintain the most reverent regard to theology, having no fears of collision because there were no points of contact. For his own part he had never been able to understand that position. It seemed to him there were, and must be, various points of contact between theology and science, and therefore frequent danger of collision, and he considered it was foolish to ignore or deny that. No doubt science and religion did revolve in different orbits, but those orbits cut one another at certain points. God spoke to us by His Word and by His works; and while for the most part He spoke of different matters in those two His great languages, it was not always so. Sometimes He spoke about the same things in the two languages, and then we were bound to interpret the one by the other, and to be very careful that we did not misinterpret either language. Now, the origin of man was just one of those matters on which God seemed to speak in both languages. But it seemed quite possible to reconcile the theory of physical evolution in the case of man's outward organism with the dignity which, by the fiat of the Creator's will, had been bestowed upon the being whom He made to be a new creature with a splendid dowry of spiritual and intellectual powers. The boldest speculations with regard to man's origin were not inconsistent with the firmest belief in his endowment with a special gift of Godlike spiritual powers, and with a new nature incapable of death. He founded that statement upon the vast and profound distinction between the material and the spiritual in man, repudiating to the utmost those materialistic theories which would confound the two, or make the spiritual nothing else but phases and phenomena of the material. Such views he held to be refuted by the very facts of human nature, and to be opposed to all that was highest and best in our nature. He believed there was a whole region of facts which could not be rationally accounted for by any one who saw in man's nature nothing but the material. He had spoken of the misreadings of the Bible, because that was the side on which he himself was bound to be mainly on his guard. The truest votaries of science knew full well that they had to be no less on their guard against misreadings on their side. It was easy to mistake our own crude interpretations for the very voice of God. After all, we were very ignorant. The wisest were but feeling after real knowledge, and he who had learned most and knew most was generally the one who was best aware how little he knew. There was a true sort of Christian agnosticism which was nothing else but a bowing-down, in our conscious ignorance, before mysteries too vast and high for our feeble grasp. He had spoken of points in the borderland where science and religion approached each other. But was there nothing to be said of the vast regions in which there was no point of contact? Christians believed they had a whole realm of precious truths and realities wholly removed from the purview of physical research and scientific classification. By means of them people could be guided safely through a world of peril, taught to conquer a rebellious will, and purify a corrupt heart. Then they could go back to science, rich with new treasures of wisdom, strong with new life and power, worshipping not Nature but Nature's God.

Note E, *page* 138.

It has been pointed out that the period during which the Christian theology took shape was "the most calamitous which the human race has lived through in historic times." (Morison, p. 35.) How wonderful, then, that Christian theologians were so remarkably preserved from error! Even if we should find notions prevailing and expressions employed which later times could not sanction, it would be unfair to charge the Bible with theories which were imported into it and not deduced from its teaching, or to hold the Church at large responsible for doctrines which it has never formally adopted. Compare also the same writer's remarks, on pages 42 *et seq.*, on the varying conceptions of the idea of God, with the argument of the lecture.

NOTE F, *page* 145.

It will be interesting to give here some account of Darwin's views on this subject as stated by Professor Max Müller in his recently published "Science of Thought," pp. 102 *et seq.* Quoting Darwin's words, "Therefore I should infer from analogy that probably all the organic beings which have ever lived on this earth have descended from some one primordial form, into which life was first breathed," he remarks: "This is all very carefully worded, yet Darwin was not satisfied, and in later editions he has considerably altered this very paragraph. The later omission (sixth edition, p. 423) of the words 'into which life was first breathed' has been much remarked upon, as indicating on Darwin's part a surrender of a belief in some extra-natural powers. But if Darwin had really meant to surrender that belief, he would never have written the following words (Origin of Species, sixth edition, p. 421): 'I see no good reason why the views given in this volume should shock the religious feelings of any one. . . . A celebrated author and divine has written to me that he has gradually learnt to see that it is just as noble a conception of the Deity to believe that He created a few original forms capable of self-development into other and needful forms, as to believe that He organized a fresh act of creation to supply the void caused by the action of His laws.'

"If I interpret Darwin's words rightly," Professor Müller goes on, "he seems to me one of those who admit, nay, who postulate, the existence of some extra-natural cause, however much he may shrink from asserting anything regarding the mode of operation. Darwin's books require to be read carefully, and from edition to edition. Let us look at the last words of his great work on the 'Origin of Species,' which no one would suppose to have been written at random. 'There is a grandeur,' he writes, 'in this view of life with its several powers having been originally breathed [by the Creator] into a few forms, or into one; and that, whilst this planet has gone cycling on according to the fixed law of gravity, from so simple a beginning endless forms, most beautiful and most wonderful, have been and are being evolved.'

"In this passage the words 'by the Creator' were absent in the first edition, and were added in the later editions. Surely they were added with a purpose. And what could have been this purpose except to define his position as one of those who, however far their researches and speculations may lead them, feel and recognize that there is always a Beyond, whatever name we call it, — a something that, even if we call it by no name, is yet forever present and irresistible. . . .

"If Darwin, later in life, said, 'I think that generally, — and more and more as I grow older, — but not always, an agnostic would be the most correct description of my state of mind,' who, as he grows older and older, would not heartily join in these words? Surely, the more we learn what knowledge really means, the more we feel that agnosticism, in the true sense of the word, is the only possible, the only reverent, and I may add, the only Christian position, which the human mind can occupy before the Unknown and the Unknowable. And, at any rate, he had introduced those words, as we learn from his Life just published, with the remark: 'In my most extreme fluctuations I have never been an atheist in the sense of denying the existence of God.'"

NOTE G, *page* 183.

"There is nothing more opposed to religion, as it is seen in human history, than the frivolous and superficial optimism that sees nothing in it but the worship of the ideal. Religion is everywhere begotten of the astonishment with which the human mind is seized in the presence of evil and sin, and of the desire which it experiences to explain their existence, and, if possible, to destroy it. He who is not conscious of suffering any evil, who is chargeable with no fault, will care little to raise his thoughts above the interests of this life. But he who says to himself, Why should I endure these evils, and how shall I succeed in pacifying a conscience laden with sin? is already on the path of religion." (Hartmann.)

NOTE H, *page* 243.

"Meanwhile," says Mr. Cotter Morison ("Service of Man," p. 33), "the historical character of the Gospels and the Acts of the Apostles, and the genuineness of several epistles ascribed to Saint Paul, have been gravely impugned, and in the opinion of many seriously damaged; an opinion not shaken by the counter efforts of the Christian apologists. Again the fortress of theology has been surrounded and commanded by the forces at the disposal of knowledge."

If we acquit Mr. Morison of disingenuousness, we can see here only the blinding influence of inveterate prejudice. Why does the writer not state that there are at least four epistles of Saint Paul to which these remarks have no application? He must know that Baur and Hilgenfeld ("Einleitung") and Renan ("Origines") all unhesitatingly accept Romans, First and Second Corinthians, and Galatians as genuine, and for the most part pure and uncorrupt as they were written; and he ought to know that the Christian theologian, so far from feeling "surrounded" by the enemy, is quite ready to reconstruct the edifice of the faith from the materials furnished by these books.

Note I, *page* 266.

An attempt has been made to produce this theory in a narrative form in a book entitled "Philochristus,"[1] which professes to be a fourth "synoptic Gospel," ostensibly proceeding from one who was an eyewitness of the events in the history of our Lord upon earth. Instead of this work being a support to the Vision or Illusion hypothesis, it is hardly possible to imagine a

[1] Published by Macmillan (Cambridge and London), and attributed to a writer who contributed several articles in the same spirit to the "Encyclopædia Britannica."

better method of discrediting the whole theory. Let any one compare the account given by Philochristus of the appearances of Jesus after His resurrection with those which are recorded in the canonical Gospels, and he will see at once that the new "Gospel" gives precisely that support to the theory which is entirely absent from the authentic documents. The theory of illusion is immediately suggested by the book of the nineteenth century; it would never occur to the mind of any one reading the original Gospels. If the new book was a disingenuous attempt to sustain the modern theory, it certainly is an abject failure; but perhaps it was written with the design of showing the absurdity of the hypothesis. If so, it has been unusually successful.

THE END.

www.ingramcontent.com/pod-product-compliance
Lightning Source LLC
Chambersburg PA
CBHW021959220426
43663CB00007B/877